Learning, Practice and Assessment

Signposting the Portfolio

Mark Doel, Catherine Sawdon and Diane Morrison

Jessica Kingsley Publishers
London and Philadelphia

First published in the United Kingdom in 2002
by Jessica Kingsley Publishers Ltd
116 Pentonville Road
London N1 9JB, England
and
325 Chestnut Street
Philadelphia, PA 19106, USA

www.jkp.com

Copyright © Jessica Kingsley Publishers 2002

Library of Congress Cataloging in Publication Data
A CIP catalog record for this book is available from the Library of Congress

British Library Cataloguing in Publication Data
A CIP catalogue record for this book is available from the British Library

ISBN 1 85302 976 9

Printed and Bound in Great Britain by
Athenaeum Press, Gateshead, Tyne and Wear

£14.95

Contents

Part 3: Postscript

Acknowledgements

We have many people to thank for their help in developing the signposted portfolio as a model of learning and assessment. First and foremost are all the learners, at various stages of professional qualification and development, whose work with the signposted porttfolio has taught us so much about its strengths, weaknesses and potential. We would also like to thank those who have supported learners with their work on portfolios, not least those service users whose stories enrich the detail of the portfolio. We trust that their reward is an improvement in the quality of service and practice.

In terms of the genesis of signposting, we would like to acknowledge Peter Marsh's collaboration in an early prototype, developing signposts for task-centred practice portfolios. Experience of signposting has been broadened and deepened by application to some DipSW qualifying portfolios, where it has replaced competency documents. The expansion of 'description' and 'commentary' categories to the current 'description', 'analysis' and 'reflection' has been pioneered with 'PQ1' portfolios, the first requirement of the post-qualifying award in social work. We would like to thank Janet Atkinson, External Assessor, for her unswerving support and lucid observations. Thanks are due, also, to practice teaching colleagues and external assessors for the Practice Teaching Award who participated in the evolution of the tea-making analogy used in Part 1 of this book.

Mark Doel, Catherine Sawdon, Diane Morrison

*To Joan and David Doel, Bill and Margaret Cormack,
and Dorothy and Eric Morrison*

Introduction

This book is the fruit of an unusual partnership. It brings together a practitioner, a training officer and an academic. Although we have different roles and perspectives, we all share a strong commitment to continuing professional development and the improvement of services with users. One of the strengths of the partnership derives from our combined experience, not just of creating an experimental design in professional assessment, but also of using it.

Mark Doel and Catherine Sawdon have developed a system of professional assessment which uses portfolios with 'signposts'; Diane Morrison is one of many practitioners who have used it. As creators, users and assessors of signposted portfolios, we have a collective vision of this project which we hope will be interesting for all those who share our fascination with learning, practice and assessment.

Our enthusiasm about the signposted project stems from the experience of its positive impact on workers and their practice. At its heart is the Groupwork Project, which is helping to establish a groupwork service in a mainstream English social services department. The project involves practitioners at various stages in their professional development, from sections throughout the agency. There are many components to the project, and the model of groupwork practice and the training curriculum have already been presented elsewhere (Doel and Sawdon 1995, 1999a, 1999b). In this book we have the opportunity to explore in more detail the ways in which practitioners enhance their learning of practice by describing, analysing and reflecting on it, for purposes of assessment. We chart a holistic approach to learning, practice and assessment which, while acknowledging the tensions between them, also demonstrates their compatibility.

Signposting

Learning, practice, assessment – these are large and potentially daunting issues, and we know that we have only scratched the surface of a large literature. However, there is less literature in respect of how learning, practice and assessment are to be integrated, and less still about the workings of this integration. While not wishing to minimize the difficulties of reconciling learning and assessment, not least the power imbalance between learner and assessor, we believe that assessors have a responsibility to use their power to create structures and signage to guide learners. After all, we anticipate encountering reliable signs when we travel around the physical landscape, so we should also expect them on our journeys into professional practice.

We will explain and demonstrate 'signposting' in the pages ahead. For now, let us note that those who compile a signposted portfolio report positively on its impact on their learning and practice; assessors, too, find it provides a telling picture to guide their judgement.

In developing the theory and practice of signposting with portfolios, we have been motivated by a commitment to two sets of values which are often seen as opposing. The first is the value of self-directed learning, creativity and innovation; and the second is the value of structure, guidance and direction. It has been a source of great delight that the signposted portfolio, though still a work in progress, seems to 'square this circle'. It generates the kind of detail which competency approaches aim for, while eliciting a broader, critical reflection of practice; though the balance alters from individual to individual, the signage in the portfolio serves to maintain a reasonable equilibrium. The signposted portfolio shapes its author's understanding in ways which promote further learning and, we hope, better practice.

Considering the growth of portfolios in nursing as well as social work, we have yet to find a way to make use of this accumulating experience, to transform it into an accessible library. Hull and Redfern (1996, p.6) muse that 'perhaps the nursing and midwifery text books of the future will be comprised of extracts from the profiles [portfolios] of reflective practitioners'. The common structure of signposted portfolios has the potential to share and compare working practices, for the benefit of all. Although it is a social work collaboration, we are confident that the messages and materials in this book are relevant to all who work in health, welfare and social care. Already, signposting has been used successfully at pre-qualifying and post-qualifying levels, and with practitioners working with a wide variety of client groups in many specialist settings. The focus of the exemplar in Part 2 is groupwork practice, but the signage can be modified to accommodate other topics and working practices. The signposting model is a generic one, which can be adapted to different contexts; the signage itself will change, but not the system of signposting.

Structure of the book

In presenting the theory and practice of signposting, we have two main aims. One is to set the signposted portfolio on a broader canvas, and the other is to show its workings in detailed practice. The structure of the book reflects these aims. We have taken the uncommon, perhaps unique, step of building the book around the reproduction of an entire portfolio (Part 2). It is presented as an exemplar; one illustration of how the signposted portfolio has been used. It needs to be read in conjunction with the other parts of the book: a consideration of holistic approaches to learning, practice and assessment (Part 1), and a postscript which reflects on the signposted portfolio and relates it to current issues in professional education (Part 3).

The portfolio in Part 2 has been slightly modified for publication, to take account of recent improvements in the signposting system. All personal and place names have been changed, except those of the authors. For practical reasons, the video extract and appendices are not included.

Other themes

The book is also a collaboration of practice and theory. This is less of an allusion to the authorship (two based in agencies, one in college), than to the content and approach of the book itself. We are aware that the good intention of 'integrating theory and practice' often seems to elude illustration. Transposing the odd preposition ('theory *in* practice', etc.) does little to settle the suspicion that theory and practice are generally conceived as oil and vinegar, in need of a vigorous shaking to mix, with the certain knowledge that they will too readily separate back out! The signposted portfolio aims to encourage theory-informed practice as well as theorizing from practice. We hope that the book itself illustrates an integration of practice and theory.

There are a number of other themes in the book which are linked by the motif of integration. We will not rehearse these themes here, but rather link them together with a notion of triples. The circles in Figure 1 illustrate the themes which have so regularly presented themselves to the authors as a recurring trio of notions, including the more tangible troika of authors and tripartite structure for the book.

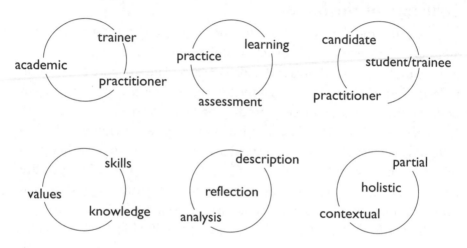

Figure 1 Themes in threes

The learner

A rose might indeed smell as sweet by any other name, but the terms we use to describe certain roles, jobs and positions carry subliminal messages. Do your teeth set on edge when you are described as a customer rather than a passenger by the 'train manager'? In social work there is still an uneasy truce around the transition from client to service user.

Against this background we have thought carefully about what to call the person who compiles a portfolio and submits it for assessment. Terms like student/trainee, practitioner, and candidate are each closely associated with learning, practice and assessment respectively. The topic of the sign-posted portfolio in this book is groupwork, and in this respect those completing a portfolio will expect to learn about groupwork as *students or trainees*, to practise groupwork as *practitioners*, and to present evidence of accomplishment in groupwork as *candidates*. Since it is the overlap between these three roles which concerns us, we want to find a term which suggests an integration of all three (see Figure 2).

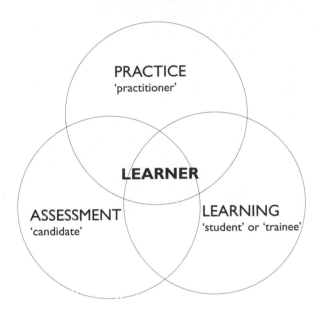

Figure 2 The learner

We have landed on the term 'learner'. It is not ideal. It is strongly associated with one of the three elements in particular (learning), and could suggest a person with 'L' plates. Nevertheless, we think it best describes the person embarking on the journey of continuing professional education. We use it throughout the book, not to imply inexperience or ineptitude, but to emphasize the critical importance of seeing ourselves as continuing learners, no matter how senior or capable.

PART 1

Integrating learning, practice and assessment

Chapter 1

Introduction to Part 1

Becoming and being a professional practitioner is highly complex. It is full of paradox, too, since the more we learn about this process, the more we learn how much more there is to learn. Moreover, this journey of professional self-discovery takes place at a time when the activities of the professions are under greater public scrutiny than ever before. The professions in Britain have experienced a fall in public confidence at the same time as an inflation in public expectations. Within the professions themselves, self-questioning can become self-doubt.

This is indeed a challenging environment in which to embark on the adventure of becoming and being a professional, especially in a spirit of open and honest enquiry. Nevertheless, these conditions are an improvement on the mystique and deference which previously shrouded the professions. The uncovering of professional malpractice and the 'discovery' of social phenomena such as child sexual abuse are not signs of a worsening state of affairs, but of a more observant and honest civic environment. Though the breath of fresh air may seem in danger of escalating into a storm force wind, this is an exciting time to embark on the adventure of becoming and being a professional; an interesting quest both for those just embarking on the journey and for those long into it. Indeed, maintaining this spirit of quest is a central element in being a practitioner. Our hope for this book is that it can be a source of encouragement and guidance, wherever you are on that journey.

In Part 1 we investigate this notion of professional practice in more detail, especially the ways in which it can be learned and assessed. A recurring theme during this first part is the complex relationship between learning and assessment, and our attempts to integrate learning, practice and assessment. We will consider the different approaches that have been taken to understand these issues, in particular those that we characterize as *'partial'* and those we characterize as *'holistic'*. By reframing some of these concepts, we hope to arrive at an integrated approach which reflects the uncertainties of practice.

In considering how these abstract ideas can find concrete expression, we arrive at the potential of portfolios, and more particularly, portfolios with 'signposts'. We explore the principles and factors which might underpin a portfolio system of learning and assessment, in preparation for the reader to move into Part 2, an example of a signposted portfolio which has been successfully completed.

Chapter 2

Professional Practice

As we noted in the preface, threes are a recurring theme in this book, and the first example is the classic trio of skills, values and knowledge.

Skills: honing personal skills into professional ones

Professional skills are, by and large, an extension of personal and interpersonal ones. They have their foundation in basic, human communication. In principle, this should make them easier to develop, but paradoxically the opposite can be true. Good interpersonal skills are significant for many occupations and do not necessarily point towards a career in social work or health care. They are not, therefore, exclusive to these professions. Whereas high wire trapeze artists show their skill very visibly and in ways which are notably different from our everyday experience, professional skills are actually at their most successful when they are not self-evidently on display. This allows careless observers to conclude (as Margaret Thatcher did in the 1980s) that the unemployed should 'do social work', with the implicit assumption that anybody can do it. Even if it was considered a socially useful passtime, unemployed people would never be exhorted to be trapeze artists, because it is manifest how very advanced and different their skills are from those we use every day.

'Let them do social work!' hits a nerve because there is a grain of truth in the prospect. Just as parents can teach their children, and friends can nurse one another, so there are elements of other professional practices, such as social work, which citizens can practise, with or without the appropriate qualification. One of the tenets of classical social work practice, 'building a relationship', is undoubtedly one of the key aspects of being a human being. This close association between the personal and the professional presents a challenge to define what is special and qualitatively different about professional skills.

The range of skills expected of many practitioners has expanded enormously. Time spent using interpersonal skills is crowded by an expanding bureaucracy of form-filling and often defensive record keeping. Increasingly, staff are expected to have sophisticated administrative skills and to be fully computer literate, too. Additional pressure from the volume of legislation, national standards and agency procedures means that self-management skills have become essential for survival. Space to reflect upon the whole range of other skills (Thompson 1995, p.97) is a rare commodity for many frontline workers and their managers.

Values: being, as well as becoming, a professional

Professional practice draws on our personal value base. The trapeze artists' abilities on the high wire are unaffected by the beliefs they hold with regard to structural oppression, personal freedoms, social responsibilities and the like. In contrast, being aware of our value base and its impact on our work is a central aspect of being a professional. We cannot leave our beliefs and values behind, any more than trapeze artists can cut loose from their sense of balance. Nevertheless, a sense of self-belief is crucial for all.

In many cases, professions require members to subscribe to an explicit value base, spelled out in a professional code of practice. Such codes must try to square the circle of enforcing strict standards of behaviour while allowing for diversity in beliefs and orientation. Individuals wishing to enter a profession will need to consider the match between their personal set of values and the profession's code. For some, reflecting on their own values will be a new and challenging experience in itself. Does the individual consider his or her personal values to be relative or immutable?

Historical evidence suggests that what we value does shift over time and that the dominant professional values have also transformed. There is an evident change of values from the emphasis on the individual, embodied in person-centredness (Rogers 1961), to a greater awareness of community, and the social and political contexts of practice (Bailey and Brake 1975; Dominelli 1988; Thompson 1993). The humanistic values of

the 1960s have not disappeared, eclipsed in some fashion by the importance of culture and diversity; rather we believe that an integration of these
apparently diverse schools of thought is both possible and necessary.

Practitioners need to consider the impact of changes in broader, social
values on professional values – for example, the move away from deferen-
tial attitudes towards people in the professions towards an emphasis on
users' rights as consumers of services. Attitudes to alcohol in the workplace
have altered radically, and values which are often considered inalienable,
such as confidentiality and privacy, are also subject to changes in interpretation and working practice; for example, the increasing belief that
employers have the right to act on employees' behaviours outside the
workplace. All of this is likely to have an impact, too, on a profession's
self-image (Gould and Harris 1996).

It is critical that practitioners understand and appraise the ways in
which their values, culture, gender, socialization and professional training
shape the beliefs they take into their work, so that they do not become
'boxed in by their own bias' (Preston-Shoot and Agass 1990, p.8).

Questioning: 'the Knowledge'

When we speak of doing a professional job, we are also making reference
to an extended knowledge base. Foundation disciplines and specific theoretical orientations help practitioners to make better sense of the world; in
the case of social workers, a knowledge of the core disciplines of sociology,
social policy and psychology underpin theoretical perspectives borrowed
by and specific to social work practice. Moreover, we expect professionals
to develop a particular kind of 'working knowledge' which takes them
beyond understanding and into application (Eraut 1994). In contrast, high
wire trapeze artists do not need a knowledge of geometry or aerodynamics
to complete a set of manoeuvres which might, nevertheless, require
complex geometric and aerodynamic theory to be explained. Indeed,
focusing on these theories would most likely put them off their stride.
However, 'acrobats have one advantage…they have to know what they are
doing; otherwise, they break their necks'! (Hesse 1979, pp.151–152).

Unlike 'the Knowledge' which taxi drivers must acquire before being
let loose on the punters of London, the body of professional knowledge is
not well-mapped or defined. Practitioners looking for an A–Z to index

and access the necessary knowledge will be frustrated, though useful first steps have been taken by Davies (2000), and Thomas and Pierson (1995). 'The Knowledge' is only one aspect of the taxi driver's cognizance; in addition to this formal body of knowledge, they develop practice wisdom associated with the best routes, depending on the time of day, the day of the week, and the flow of traffic. This uncodified knowledge is not found in the London A–Z, but it has just as much significance. Professional practitioners, too, rely on developing this kind of informal knowledge of the local scene, a kind of practice wisdom where knowledge becomes manifest rather than 'a given', and working hypotheses are made explicit. In this way, knowledge becomes less of a product and more of a process (Lyons 2000, p.435).

This informal knowledge can become semi-codified into what has long been known as practice theory (Curnock and Hardiker 1979). Just as taxi drivers develop working theories to explain the ebb and flow of the traffic, so practitioners make sense of their immediate experiences by collecting a number of related hypotheses into practice theories; they do this as part of the web of information and experience which is shared between them. Thus, the knowledge and theory used in practice is practitioner-led, implicit and developed through experiential learning – 'reflection -in-action' (Schön 1987, 1995).

Much of the knowledge which practitioners draw from is tacit, presumed rather than stated (Meerabeau 1992), so that values and existing skills shape the practitioner's knowledge in ways which are not necessarily known to them. If all you have in your tool kit is a hammer, problems requiring a hammer become highly valued; indeed, every problem comes to be defined as a nail! Learning is concerned with finding ways of helping tacit knowledge become manifest, so that it can be open to critical appraisal.

Social work, in particular, has a perspective which takes account of the whole, and this requires a broad knowledge; not only the taxi driver's street level knowledge, but also the bus routes, the underground lines, the utilities' plans, the air space grid and, crucially, the relationship between them all. Moreover, the process of discovery of this knowledge also changes it in a reflexive way: 'by their understanding of the ambiguous nature of social knowledge…social workers necessarily become entwined in the value systems and objectives of their clients' (Payne 1996, p.158).

Social work draws from bodies of knowledge which are large, fluid and frequently contested, and what constitutes knowledge is itself highly politicized. Returning to our taxi driver analogy, it is as if powerful groups had a vested interest in declaring parts of the taxi driver's Knowledge 'no-go' areas or simply unfashionable. Concerns that certain areas of practice knowledge might become 'no-go' help explain the tension between the drive for national standards on the one hand and professional autonomy on the other.

Setting all this in context

All practitioners work in a political context, though some see their role as specifically political, others less so. Social work, for example, involves the most marginalized groups in society and has long considered the political dimension of professional practice (Jordan and Parton 1983), embracing notions of power and oppression in its practice (Thompson 1998). As professions have been increasingly brought to account for their activities, so the directly political environment in which they operate has become more transparent to all. Even those forces which have generally denied this relationship have been increasingly prepared to make it explicit, to the extent that the direct link between levels of taxation and the funding of professional practitioners was made manifest even by conservative forces in the 2001 UK general election ('You paid the tax, so where are the teachers?').

Professional practice in the twenty-first century is in a very different place from the twentieth, and the curriculum will need to reflect these changes if newly qualifying people are to practise successfully in these changed circumstances. Professionally-led definitions of service are being replaced by consumer-led ones (Jones and Joss 1995); these, in turn, are increasingly being overshadowed by definitions driven by central government. Whereas professionalism has been a means for occupational control, it is increasingly defined in terms of fitness to do a particular job to a national standard, and what is 'fit' is less likely to be defined by the occupational group itself. Broader access to knowledge and information also means that professional groups can no longer claim exclusive grasp on an esoteric knowledge base; with an internet connection, it is the patient who is likely to be informing the doctor of the latest treatments and self-help groups.

Chapter 3

Learning Professional Practice

How does the fledgling become the professional and maintain that professionalism? In other words, how is practice learnt and how do we know whether the learning is taking place and whether it is being successful? When is one method of learning, such as enquiry and action learning (Burgess and Jackson 1991; Burgess 1992) more or less effective than another, such as simulated learning (Doel and Shardlow 1996)? What do we know about the best methods to help transfer learning from the training environment to practice itself (Garavaglia 1993), or the significance of tutoring and coaching (Huczynski 1989)? How do combinations of these and other approaches work?

These are complex questions with no easy answers. Rather like the value base of the social work profession, which we described earlier as transforming over time, the dominant models that have been used to understand how newcomers learn their trade have also evolved (Doel *et al.* 1996, p.4). Knowles (1978) attempted to identify characteristics of individual adult learners and to link this directly to guidance about how learning may be facilitated. He questioned prevailing didactic models of teaching and increased the learner's power within the learning process. Humphries (1988) challenged these assumptions as based on Knowles' own values as a white, middle-class, male academic, and pointed to the direct impact of context and structural factors on the learning process, rather than focusing on individual learners' strengths and deficits. This was a fundamental change, whose roots can be found in the works of Freire (1972, p.55); 'authentic reflection considers neither abstract man [sic] nor the world without man, but men in their relations with the world'. From this perspective, learning is seen as active and dynamic; not just thinking, but doing, too (Gibbs 1988).

We do not have space to explore these many different models and critiques, but Figure 3 illustrates how different models have different preoccupations: the content of the learning, the process of the learning, or the attributes of the learner.

- teacher is expert
- learner is recipient
- knowledge is given

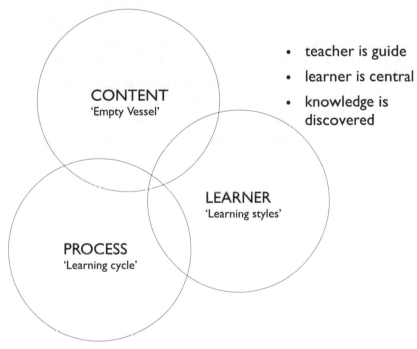

- teacher is guide
- learner is central
- knowledge is discovered

CONTENT
'Empty Vessel'

LEARNER
'Learning styles'

PROCESS
'Learning cycle'

- teacher is facilitator
- learner is participent
- knowledge is experienced

Figure 3 The focus of models of learning

At its extreme, the focus on *content* is represented by the 'empty vessel' model of learning, in which learners are considered to be the blank CD on which the profession's wisdom is to be burned. This is a deeply unfashionable view, and few espouse it explicitly. However, it is typical for quangos charged with the responsibility for professional education to focus on content and to equate the notion of curriculum with content alone. Most training curricula continue to be content driven. For all the rhetoric, then, content remains a strong preoccupation.

Those models that focus on the *processes* of learning are likely to emphasize the technology or dynamics of how we learn, and attempt to arrive at a general theory or explanation of learning applicable to all. Reynolds' (1942) stages of learning is an early example of a model which focuses on the processes of learning. Boud, Keogh and Walker (1985) identify three stages of reflective learning. However, the best known example is Kolb's (1984; see Figure 4). This is not a linear process, but a cycle which might begin with concrete experience, specifically focused either on learning or life experiences in general. The model considers that it is essential to reflect on the experience and its significance, in order to make sense of it and to learn from it. Reflective observation leads to greater consideration of the issues arising from this experience. Links can be made to other experiences, beliefs and attitudes and integrated into our overall life experience. Such conceptualizing often means forming a working hypothesis. The fourth stage of the cycle is that of active experimentation, at which point the new learning is tried out in practice, and learning at an abstract level is translated into the concrete reality of practice. This completes a cycle and begins a new one, as the active experimentation becomes the concrete experience of a new cycle.

Other models of learning focus on the learner. They emphasize the fact that we are not blank sheets and we have learned different ways of learning. Adult learners in particular have considerable life experiences which influence their attitude to learning and new experiences. Their personal biography, as a man or a woman, as a black person or a white person, has a significant bearing on their approach and response to learning. Individual learners may face significant blocks or barriers to their learning, and models of learning must take account of these differences.

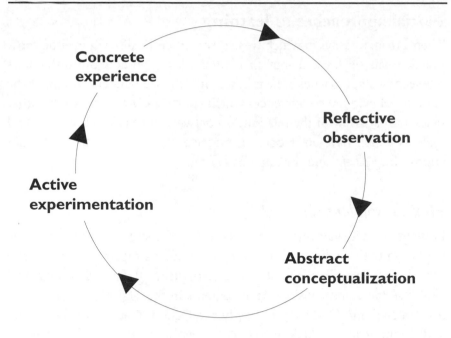

Figure 4 Kolb's learning cycle

An example of the focus on the learner is Honey and Mumford's (1986) learning styles. This consists of a questionnaire to reveal the individual learner's learning profile, which is a score allocated to each of four different approaches to learning: activist; reflector; theorist; pragmatist. It is important not to apply labels, but to use the model to help learners to identify if they have preferred learning styles. The questionnaire has often been used to justify the idea of matching style to method of learning, though it could be just as useful to encourage learners to extend their repertoire of learning styles. The notion of repertoire is a key component of professional practice (Jones and Joss 1995; Sawdon and Sawdon 1988).

There are, of course, areas of overlap between these three approaches. For instance, Kolb's learning cycle has a link with learning styles, too, since we can enter the cycle at our preferred point.

Partial approaches to learning

There are many ways in which we can construct the discussion about how practice can be learned, but this often hinges around the differences between two approaches. One is based on a detailed understanding of the various behavioural competences which constitute practice, and the other takes a broad view of the relationship between the various processes and systems which have an impact on practice. We will refer to the former approach as *partial* and the latter as *holistic*.

How do you take your tea?

Perhaps we can gain more understanding of these two approaches by exploring their application in a different context altogether. From time to time during Part 1, we will ask you to step outside the world of social and health services and consider developments in the Training Organization for Tea-Making (TOTEM). Formerly the Central Council for Education and Training in Tea-Making, TOTEM has been established to develop good practice in tea-making, and has decided that the best way to help student tea-makers develop sound practice is to consider the question 'What makes for a good cup of tea?' The answer to this simple question should also provide guidance about how to assess the learner as a tea-maker. If we know what a good cup of tea is, we can then know whether tea-making students are able to make a professional cup of tea sufficient for the award of the DipTM.

TOTEM sent the question 'What makes for a good cup of tea?' out for consultation and began to categorize the responses along various criteria. For example:

- Some people liked their tea milky, others with just a drop, yet others with none.
- Some took sugar, honey or other sweeteners, others took no sweeteners.
- Some liked it strong, others weak, and so on.

These various preferences help to develop indicators to map a good cup of tea. So, a criterion of 'sweetness' covers those who would include sugar and those who would not. 'Strength', 'milkiness', 'brewing time', and other criteria could be similarly developed, like pieces in a jigsaw which together make up a picture of the factors which contribute to TOTEM's understanding of a good cup of tea.

Identifying the various elements which constitute a good cup of tea enables TOTEM to partialize something which is complex. This, in turn, enables fledgling tea-makers to take a step-by-step approach to develop their tea-making abilities. The consultation exercise has also alerted TOTEM to the necessary subjectivity of 'a good cup of tea', and the fact that one person's nectar is another's dishwater. Each element could be presented as a continuum, and an individual's preference mapped along each one.

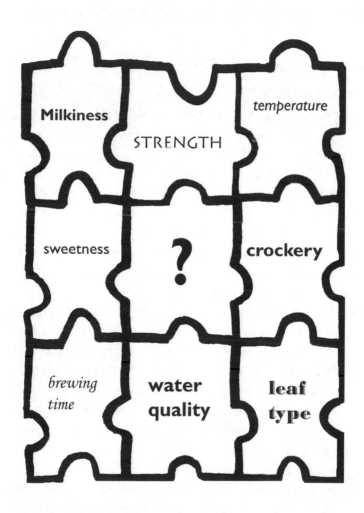

Figure 5 Learning to make 'a good cup of tea'

To summarize, partial approaches are those which break down a complex activity into smaller parts to help us understand these separate elements and learn them more easily. This has its philosophical roots in Cartesian dualism, with its notion of separateness, otherness and discrete identities. In more recent years, behavioural psychology has developed methods of learning, unlearning and re-learning, using partial approaches. (See 'Signposts' in Doel and Shardlow 1998, pp.203–206 for an example of partializing the elements which influence practitioners' decisions.)

We have considered the partial approach to learning and illustrated it with reference to the way a student might learn professional tea-making. What, then, do we understand by holistic approaches to learning?

Holistic approaches to learning

Law of excluded middle

The dominant model of Western philosophy and thought tends to dichotomy, that is, to see the world in terms of opposites: as this or that; black or white; good or evil. Indeed, when knowledge is digitalized it is reduced to either '0' or '1'. Language reinforces this sense of either/or: something is either here or there; either night or day; all was dark and then there was light. In philosophic logic this has been codified as the law of excluded middle, 'which states that a proposition must be either true or false, or, in other words, that it is impossible that a proposition and its contradictory should neither of them be true' or, indeed, both be true (Ayer 1946, p.76) – either P or not P (Stage 1 of Figure 6).

This polarized thinking is widespread. When considering what makes us who we are, there is a polarity between nature and nurture – explaining our make-up in terms of genetic, biological determinants on the one hand, or the products of social and environmental influences on the other. In fields of intellectual enquiry, there is a similar opposition, such as quantitative vs. qualitative in research activity; lateral or linear in ways of thinking. The bipolar approach is evident in writings about professional practice; social work as 'a *rational-technical* activity or a *practical-moral* one' (Parton 2000, p.452), practitioners as positivist or anti-reductionist (Sibeon 1999). Partial approaches and holistic approaches are similarly presented as separate camps. Like two football clubs, United or City, there are strong pressures to decide which group of supporters to join, rallying round the red or the blue.

A 'continuum' approach

In the tea-making analogy, we begin to see how the act of piecing together the jigsaw moves us towards a more complete picture of the skills needed to learn how to make tea. Each piece on its own is a partial understanding of the process, yet taken together we get a better understanding of the whole. This leads us to a softening of the polar opposites we described earlier as P or -P (not P). Instead, we begin to conceptualize approaches to learning as perhaps tending to partial or tending to holistic. They do not have to be either partial or holistic, but lie somewhere along a continuum (Stage 2 of Figure 6).

Using the notion of a continuum, we can identify shades of grey between black and white; dawn and dusk between night and day. There are some approaches to learning practice which are more partial, and others which are more holistic. Perhaps we can bring together the elements of a good cup of tea (the jigsaw pieces) to move towards a view of the whole picture.

Contextualizing

The notion of a continuum is more satisfying because it is dynamic and allows for a more subtle shading of the two approaches. Nevertheless, the continuum continues to reinforce the view of two approaches which are, essentially, opposites. The continuum is more subtle, yet still fails to do justice to the complexity of professional practice and the ways in which it can be learned.

Let us return to the tea-making analogy to expand on this. We began to understand tea-making by looking at the elements which make 'a good cup of tea' and we moved on from a series of individual factors to an understanding of how they associate with each other. We could encourage the student of tea-making to see these separate elements as criteria, i.e. factors which they must consider when understanding the idea of a good cup of tea, thus providing a rudimentary framework for the student's learning.

Stage 1 – the either/or dichotomy:

Partial **or -P**artial

Stage 2 – two ends of a continuum:

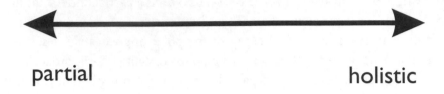

partial   holistic

Stage 3 – an integrated approach

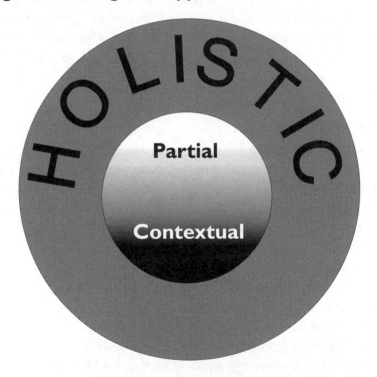

Figure 6 Reframing our understanding of 'holistic'

The student tea-maker has been focusing on issues intrinsic to the cup of tea; in other words, the focus has been the cup of tea itself, its temperature, milkiness, sweetness, etc. However, there are also factors extrinsic to the cup of tea, which have a bearing on the understanding. These factors might be very significant, perhaps more so than the ones we previously identified. For example, the company, the time of day it is drunk, who makes it, and the occasion on which it is taken may all be significant. All of these factors, and more, can influence the tea-drinker's view of quality when describing the cup of tea, though none of them are related to what goes into the cup. Some of these environmental factors will be within the tea-maker's influence, others not.

The tea-drinkers have much to contribute to the tea-maker's understanding of all of these intrinsic and extrinsic elements. These tea-users can help to add further pieces to the jigsaw. There may also be factors which few really understand or identify but which, nevertheless, are very significant in the quality of the cup of tea (the quality of the water might be rarely identified, yet could be crucial to the taste of a delicate drink like tea).

Although the widening of our enquiry to the local context helps to satisfy a need for the broader picture, we cannot yet say that we have arrived at a complete picture of 'what makes a good cup of tea'. For example, what assumptions lie behind the very act of learning how to make tea? 'A good cup of tea' is a commonplace phrase in England, and it carries many assumptions. At a simple level it assumes 'a cup', when indeed a mug, pot or samovar may be a more favoured description. At a more fundamental level, you may have no view at all about a good cup of tea because you do not drink tea. For cultural, aesthetic or other reasons, the drinking of tea is not an experience you can relate to. You are not a tea-drinker and do not wish to be one. The dominant group may be tea-drinkers, but it would be oppressive to assume that there is a universal tea-drinking experience.

Moreover, we have focused on the tea-drinker and the tea-maker without a consideration of the wider tea economy. Would it be possible to speak of a 'good' cup of tea without considering the relationships between tea-growers, tea-buyers and tea-sellers? How ethical are the policies which have made the cup of tea possible? If a cup of tea is made competently but it has been brewed on the back of exploitative trade practices, to what extent can this be considered a 'good' cup of tea?

We can see how the relatively simple question of how we might educate a person in the art and science of tea-making has revealed the complexity of levels to take into account when we consider education for professional practice. One level of understanding is gained by partializing a complex activity into its different and separate parts. This helps to acquire skills which improve performance. However, our understanding is broadened by considering the context of practice. At a local level, the factors are influenced by time and place, such as the mood of the tea-drinker and the company in which the tea is taken. At a social level, a structural analysis allows us to go deeper as well as broader. This ensures that the education of professionals includes the psychological and socio-political contexts.

Reframing our understanding of 'holistic'

It is said that because Louis Pasteur spent so much of his time peering down a microscope at the particles which make up our world, he became somewhat obsessed with the smallness of life and so troubled by the multitudes of microbes he found that he used to break up his food and crumble the bread on his plate as a part of his obsessive search. We might consider the moral of the story to be that Pasteur lost the plot; focusing on the microworld led him to forget the meaning of food, its appearance, its taste, and the social significance of taking a meal. However, what the story tells us is that we should know what our purpose is. If we want to isolate the virulent microbe which is causing lethal food poisoning, we surely need to 'crumble the food' and analyse it in fine detail. However, we will find neither the taste of the food nor the social effects of a meal taken with good company, by breaking it into crumbs. We need to know how to do both.

The ability to move between these various levels, from the partial to the context, and understand the relationship between the local and the structural, is what we understand as a holistic approach. It is misguided, therefore, to consider a holistic approach as 'the opposite' of a partial one. It is better, but still inadequate, to see a holistic approach as in a continuum with a partial approach. A holistic approach is, therefore, not one which is in opposition to a partial approach, but one which encompasses it. Partial approaches and contextual approaches are different facets of the same holistic approach. In this analysis, a holistic approach is holistic precisely because it envelops both the partial and the contextual elements. The holistic approach is not a choice but an absolute essential for professional learning and practice; partial approaches are, paradoxically, an essential ingredient of holism.

Chapter 4

Assessing Professional Practice

There are many reasons why practice must be assessed, and the most important is protection for service users. As a minimum, assessment is important in order to select out those people who are unsuitable and who might engage in the kind of dangerous practices identified by Thompson (2000, pp.129–134): routinized; defensive; defeatist; chaotic; and oppressive. However, this is only a minimum. People have a right to expect fine services, and assessment is necessary to test for the presence of good practices, not simply the absence of poor ones.

Earlier, we came to an understanding that deciding what is knowledge for professional practice is not a neutral activity. Assessment, too, is a highly political area. As well as the laudable aim of protecting service users, 'an important aspect of professional power and occupational control is the way in which access to and standards of an occupation are controlled' (Payne 1996, p.153). Professions have a vested interest in maintaining their power and credibility, and the doors to some professions swing open more readily for certain social groups than others. Rigorous assessment is also part and parcel of the competition for territory amongst and between different occupational groupings.

In addition to gatekeeping entry to the profession, assessment is necessary to maintaining the standards beyond the point of qualification. In social work and social care, the advent of a General Social Care Council and the slow but steady advance of post-qualifying and advanced awards in social work all herald a new and more systematic approach to continuing professional development, and with it continuing professional assessment. Those who manage frontline workers have a stake in the assessment of practice beyond the point of qualification, and those who define the criteria for assessment and inspection are in a powerful position of trust. We should expect safeguards, too, that managerial assessments focus properly on dangerous practices such as routinized and defeatist work, and not on practitioners who are rightly critical of poor agency policies or inept managerial practices.

Partial approaches to assessment

Good practice is increasingly being described in terms of competence. Considerable licence is taken with this word (O'Hagan 1996), and the general notion of competent practice is dissected into smaller parts, referred to as competencies or characteristics (ENB 1994).

Competency-based training may have its origins in performance-based teacher education in America in the 1960s (Velde 1999), but it is during the 1990s that it has become pre-eminent, in part a reaction to the almost cussed refusal of the professions over many years to demystify the processes of becoming a professional practitioner. There are obvious attractions to partializing assessment by developing competencies, not least the scope for incremental assessment, in which learners can acquire credit by taking one 'module' of learning at a time. As each competency is learned, so can it be assessed, step by step. The specific and discrete behavioural indicators, or learning outcomes, which have come to characterize the competency approach, enable independent others to observe whether these behaviours have been achieved or not. Competencies give assessor and assessed a sense (or is it an illusion?) of objectivity.

Where training is designed to produce conformity, perhaps to ensure safety in an industrial setting, a competency approach is likely to have a central place. Mulcahy (2000, p.261) refers to this as an instructional model of competency, where training 'involves bringing someone or something to a desired standard or state'. Competency approaches have much in common, therefore, with earlier industrial models such as apprenticeship ('sitting by Nellie'), with Nellie now replaced by a list of outcome indicators.

The partial approach to assessment has its difficulties. Is competence a behaviour, an outcome, or a personal attribute? (Velde 1999). How far do we reduce the skills, knowledge and values of practice; to the smallest behavioural tic? The reductivist approach can lead to 'Pasteurized' practice, in which events are crumbled to the extent that their meaning and essence are lost. Efforts to re-capture this sense of the whole can lead to comprehensive but burdensome bullet points of dotted 'i's and crossed 't's. 'In competency-based training, assessment tends to highlight the readily measurable, over-emphasising details, rather than promoting the essential aspects of competence' (Velde 1999, p.442).

The competency approach is of less value when we move towards what Mulcahy (2000) terms the educational model, where the focus is more on contexts than content, more on fluid, dynamic situations than fixed certainties. Moreover, the supposed objectivity of competency models has also been called into question, with a view that 'competence can only be inferred rather than observed' (Jones and Joss 1995, p.20). Clearly, there are different perspectives about what should or should not be considered a competency and how it should be assessed, and the power to decide what is competent practice and how it will be assessed is increasingly under centralized control and linked to notions of employability (Gibbs 2000), which we explore in Part 3. By keeping its eye so fixedly on the ball, the competency model is in danger of forgetting the players, the spectators and the game itself.

Holistic approaches to assessment

We have seen that partial approaches to assessment reduce good practice to its constituent elements, with each aspect examined on its own merits. In place of general judgements about 'pass' or 'fail', a partial assessment enables a consideration of which parts of the person's practice are competent and why, and which are not yet competent, and what specific improvements are needed.

The partial approach to assessment struggles to encompass the whole. Put crudely, it might count and measure every fragment of a cup and find each adequate, yet fail to notice that these broken pieces are not 'a cup'. As with learning, so assessment of practice must consider context. Professional practice relies on 'dynamic competence', the ability to integrate skills, theory and values (Manor 2000, p.209). This integration has been referred to as artistry, the art of inventing on the spot (Schön 1992). A rounded assessment of professional talents requires us to find ways of assessing these kinds of creative qualities, too.

To understand and undertake a holistic approach to assessment, the partial and the contextual must be considered together, in parallel with the process we described earlier in relation to holistic approaches to learning (Figure 6). In this way, we arrive at a synthesis of specific and general, discrete and dynamic. This is a truly holistic approach to assessment, and we will explore how this might be achieved later, with a complete exemplar of this approach presented in Part 2.

Principles to support a system of assessment

True to its philosophy of integration, a holistic approach will consider the assessment system itself as well as the individual assessments. The principles on which the assessment system is founded should be explicit, so they are open to challenge and review. Is it a competent system? The following four principles are crucial (adapted from Doel *et al.* 1996, pp.157–158).

Accurate

How reliable and valid is the assessment system in reflecting the abilities of those who are assessed? This might imply the need to devise a variety of assessment methods in order to arrive at a rounded view. An accurate system is one which avoids assessing the wrong abilities (e.g. the report-writing abilities of a supervisor mistaken for the practice abilities of a learner).

Fair

Persons training for professional practice must have confidence that the assessment system is fair. There are a number of interests to take into account, and it is proper that a balance is achieved between 'the examiner's desire for the rigorous scrutiny of practice, the students' wishes to present good examples of their work, and the interests and protection of users in the kind of service which they receive or would like to receive' (Doel *et al.* 1996, p.158). There should be an equitable balance between common standards overall and positive action to ensure that particular individuals do not face discrimination and are not disadvantaged.

Efficient

The system of assessment must take account of real limitations, such as time. If the assessment system consumes an unacceptable proportion of time, it will fall into disrepute. Costly or cumbersome systems will trigger shortcuts which can undermine the integrity of the system as a whole. It is crucial to learn how to choose samples of work in order to lighten the potential load of assessment.

Authentic

A central theme of this book is the relationship between learning and assessment. We believe that the two processes are neither separate nor in opposition; they are interlinked in a complex dynamic. The system of assessment should, therefore, consider the affinity between learning and assessment. In short, it should be authentic. How might some methods of assessment enhance learning and others inhibit it? What system and methods of assessment will encourage the best 'fit' between the learning, the practice and the examination of that practice? For example, the driving test could be faulted for testing the learner's ability to behave as expected for a driving test, rather than everyday driving behaviour.

A system of assessment for 'TOTEM'

Let us return to the consultation exercise introduced in Chapter 3 and undertaken by TOTEM, the Training Organization for Tea-Making, to consider how these principles could be incorporated into its system of assessment.

Accurate – We need to feel confident of a rounded and accurate picture of the candidates' overall abilities. For example, if tea-makers were expected to make a cup of tea under test conditions, to video tea-users in discussion and reflect on this in a viva voce, and to write an assignment on fair trade in tea production, this could provide a sufficient variety of sources of evidence to be assured of the accuracy of any judgement.

Fair – If the assessment included making a cup of tea under examination conditions, we would expect a blind student to have access to specialized equipment which sounds a buzzer when water is approaching the rim of the cup. We would expect external assessors to ensure that the Tea-Making Award was not easier to achieve on one course than another.

Efficient – If the novices were competent in tea-making in two or three different circumstances, the assessment system should allow us to deduce that they would be able to transfer this learning to other untested areas. Experience would teach the assessors which particular circumstances were the most reliable in making this deduction.

Authentic – If the student were required to provide evidence for the assessment consisting of research into what tea-drinkers most appreciate in a cup of tea, the very process of this enquiry would fit the student well for future practice. This is a reflexive process, in which the assessment, the learning and the practice feed back into each other.

Assessment at different levels

The same system of assessment can be used to determine aptitudes at very different levels. For example, the nursing profession in the UK uses ten key characteristics, requiring nurses to demonstrate safe practice at the first level, safe and effective practice at the second, and safe, effective and efficient practice at the third, with specified learning outcomes (ENB 1994).

With tea-making, TOTEM might decide to begin with a partial approach, examining the learner's ability to break a task into smaller, more manageable parts and to reproduce the correct behaviours, the mechanics of preparing and brewing a single cup of tea. At the next level, learners might be expected to understand that there are different understandings of 'a good cup of tea'. A learner able to use predefined criteria could be considered to be operating at a basic level, and one capable of developing new criteria in the light of experience and enquiry to be more advanced. A step further, we could assess the capacity to find out about various tea drinkers' personal preferences and the know-how to respond to these. Learners would be expected to be questioning their own attitudes towards tea-drinking.

Take this a stage further and we begin to assess the ability to conceptualize these separate and individual preferences as criteria, and to bring these criteria together into an overall understanding of tea-making: a rudimentary theory of tea-making. An assessor would not be looking for a definitive 'good cup of tea'. Indeed, a learner with a definite view of a good cup of tea would be failing one of the fundamental principles: the understanding that this is a relative concept.

Beyond this, our assessment could relate to the learner's understanding of contrasting theories of tea-making, an awareness of the broader cultural meaning of tea-drinking and the significance of socio-political analyses of the wider tea economy. At an advanced level, we might expect evidence of proficiency at influencing some of these contextual factors.

A holistic assessment of learners would bring together the partial approach (essentially, can they reproduce the necessary skills to make effective cups of tea in different circumstances?) and the contextual approach (essentially, are they able to reflect on the factors which have an impact on the lives of tea-growers, tea-sellers and tea-buyers as well as tea-drinkers?). Those hoping to practise the art and science of tea-making would reflect on all of these processes in order to become autonomous, self-critical tea-makers.

A holistic approach requires a system of assessment which is inclusive and less culturally defined than one which is confined to competencies. What is unclear is how this relates to levels and standards of practice. Is holistic practice an advanced form, which follows an initial grasp of competencies, or is it possible, even necessary, to learn holistic practice at beginning, intermediate and advanced stages of development? We have opinions about this, but not a lot of knowledge.

Chapter 5

Learning and Assessing

With the memory of the driving test, we can be quick to presume that the process of assessment inhibits learning. Performance deteriorates because of anxiety about the possibility of failure; or performance is tailored in special ways to 'second guess' the assessor. For example, despite the qualitative differences between students' ability to reflect, Boud and Knights (1996, p.31) do not feel that reflection should be graded, for fear that those assessed might give the kind of response they surmise the assessor is seeking, rather than an honest reflection of their uncertainty. However, we might just as well presume that candidates sophisticated in these matters would seek to please assessors by implying a sense of uncertainty where, in fact, they felt none! Far from detrimental to performance, it could be that the awareness of assessment improves it. The nature of the relationship between assessment and learning cannot be assumed, but it is clear that there is a complex relationship between the two.

A holistic approach to learning and assessment

Earlier we reframed the competency vs. holistic dualism. We explored the way in which the holistic approach has been unhelpfully tethered at the end of a continuum, opposite the partial approach (which, itself, has become singly identified with competencies). By seeing this supposed opposite as a contextual approach, we can use the concept of holism to encompass both the partial and contextual approaches, as two sides to the same coin rather than opposite ends of a continuum (Figure 6). The abilities to partialize and contextualize are of reciprocal importance, with no benefit from establishing opposing camps, nor from compromised positions halfway along this flawed continuum. A holistic approach provides us with a synthesis.

If we are to develop a holistic approach to learning and assessment, we must ensure that the partial and contextual approaches are in balance. There are examples of attempts of this kind, such as Winter and Maisch's (1996) ASSET programme, described as 'an attempt to bridge notions of competence, on the one hand, and artistry on the other' (Yelloly and Henkel 1995, pp.61–62). The outcomes and the cognitive processes must be linked, so that 'the role of judgement in performance, based upon the formation of process knowledge, becomes central in a holistic approach' (Jones and Joss 1995, p.28). The holistic approach integrates learning and assessment, and this is built into the design of the curriculum and the assessment protocol, so that there is congruence between them.

Learners need to be able to describe their work in clear detail. Presenting succinct accounts of professional practice is useful learning as well as important evidence for assessment. Knowing how to take representative and illuminating samples of practice, and learning how to convey them in a 'factual' manner is an important skill which demonstrates the learner's ability at a partial level. The learner might choose to describe a range of events, demonstrating expected and unexpected events, planned and improvised responses.

Having presented samples of work at a descriptive level, learners need to be able to analyse their practice. What meanings do they attribute to the practice which they have described? Practitioners should be able to consider why events unfolded as they did, and what part they played in these events. This commentary provides learners with the opportunity to make judgements and observations. Learners set their practice in a broader context, using theories and working hypotheses to provide explanations, investigating the possible impact of policies and procedures and making tentative associations with other aspects of their practice. The learner's critique should demonstrate the ability to make connections.

Above all, the holistic approach emphasizes reflection. Learners should have a capacity to reflect on the work which they have described and analysed, speculating on how past experiences relate to their present understanding, and what changes they might make in the light of any new understanding. Mezirow (1981, 1990) describes this as a process of 'per-

spective transformation', in which practitioners challenge their precon-
ceptions and release themselves from being hidebound by limiting beliefs
created by past experiences. When reflecting on their practice, learners can
disclose their feelings, too: feelings 'then' (at the time of the practice previously described) and 'now', and any insights they have developed. The
process of reflection enables learners to consider their continuing needs as
learners, in the light of their current practice. They step to the side of
themselves in order to obtain a different view of their own learning and
practice, eventually consolidating new knowledge as a part of how they
act and feel (Boud *et al.* 1985).

Although it is proper to be critical of any notion which has become an
orthodoxy, as reflective practice has (Ixer 1999), we hope that it is clear
from the preceding paragraphs that there are qualitative differences
between description, analysis and reflection. 'The reflective practitioner is
essentially a holistic model...it is not only concerned with the outcomes of
professional practice but the cognitive processes by which these are developed and demonstrated' (Jones and Joss 1995, p.28). This combination of
description, analysis and reflection provides an integrated approach to
learning and assessment (see Figure 7 and Davies and Sharp (2000, p.69)
for parallels in nursing practice). We conclude Part 1 by considering how
this might be developed in practice using a portfolio framework.

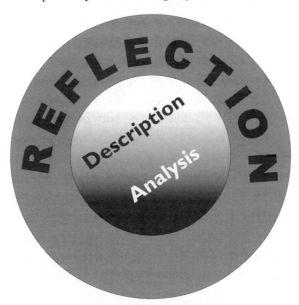

Figure 7 An integrated approach to the portfolio

What is a portfolio?

Conduct a literature search on 'portfolio' and you are just as likely to find materials on art, finance, historical documents, photographic anthologies, articles on estate management and folders of musical exercises, as information about professional education. It has itself become a 'portfolio' term – transferable, flexible, updatable. It is both an abstract idea and a concrete tool.

There are, then, various kinds of portfolio. For some, it is synonymous with 'work-book' (Walker 1985, p.53); for others, it is 'a purposeful collection of a learner's work that tells the story of their efforts, progress and achievements' (Hellman 1999, p.216), 'a kind of autobiography of growth' (Jarvinen and Kohonen 1995, p.29). Nursing portfolios have achieved a central importance and the vast engine of profiling in nursing has become commercial, with glossy (and expensive) portfolio structures available for purchase (Brown 1995). When we consider the portfolio in social work, however, Taylor, Thomas and Sage (1999, p.148) observe that 'given its widespread use, there is surprisingly little critical analysis of its application'.

If individual portfolios differ enormously, so do the systems which underpin them. There are a wide variety of structures used to assess the portfolio (individual assessors, panels, viva voces, etc). The criteria used, the methods for channelling feedback and the range of outcomes of assessment are, again, disparate. The amount of support (via a mentor or line manager) available to portfolio writers varies, as does the availability of written and verbal guidance from programmes. Some systems will require little more than a written assignment, while others will ask for a true portfolio of materials; that is, a collection of evidence using a variety of media, which could include audiotape, video, flipchart sheets, letters, questionnaires and more.

Assessment systems using portfolios need to be aware of the potential for discrimination, too; for example, against learners with sensory impairments or dyslexia. It is important to be clear who owns which parts of a portfolio. Nursing portfolios contain both public and private sections, though the large majority of what is included in the portfolio is public. The identity of sources for evidence must be protected and issues of confidentiality considered, including the question of whether material in the portfolio could be used as evidence in court (Hull and Redfern 1996).

So, with this enormous variety of portfolio systems and formats, what do they have in common? The following features, highlighted by an early experiment in the use of portfolios, remain relevant:

- Explicit commitment to developing assessment methods which are congruent with learning.

- Emphasis on the direct voice of the learner, rather than mediation via an expert witness such as the supervisor, so that the learners are the authors of their own assessment materials.

- Variety of media used to collect evidence, to obtain a rounded and more accurate view of practice ability, and to counter discrimination (e.g. not relying solely on a person's writing skills).

(Doel and Shardlow 1989)

The notion of congruency between learning and assessment has developed greater significance, especially with the growth in our understanding of reflective learning. Additionally, the emphasis on a variety of media enables learners to present 'performance evidence' as well as 'product evidence' (Rhodes and Tallantyre 1999); that is, evidence that can be judged by observation, perhaps via a video-tape, as well as evidence where assessors make inferences about abilities. Although the portfolios in Doel and Shardlow's (1989) study were completed over the course of one student placement, portfolios have increasingly been seen as work in progress, whose compilers collect evidence of their continuing development throughout their careers. Rather like an artist's portfolio, it should be possible to witness the individual practitioner's growth in style and expertise.

An integrated portfolio system

We believe the portfolio has the potential to achieve the kind of integrity of learning and assessment which we are exploring in this book. However, given the vagueness of the term 'portfolio', it is necessary to identify a number of factors which are key to this process.

Principles

First, the portfolio system needs to be based on explicit principles which include:

AN AUTHENTIC FIT BETWEEN LEARNING AND ASSESSMENT

The programme should have an explicit commitment to consider what positive or negative impact the assessment of practice has on the learning of that practice. To what extent do the assessment arrangements and methods make it possible for the 'learning hand' to fit into the 'assessment glove', so that the learning is reinforced by the assessment, rather than inhibited by it? It is not possible to create an exact fit, nor a fit that is common to every individual, but integration of learning and assessment is more likely in a programme which is asking itself these questions.

ASSESSMENT WHICH EMPOWERS

There is an inherent power differential between assessor and assessed. Learners submit their work to assessment systems which have the power to make judgements, and these judgements can find the learner wanting. Similar imbalances are to be found in practitioners' own work, where they are expected to develop empowering partnerships with service users, clients and patients. How can the assessment arrangements and methods ensure that learners experience the assessment as one which leaves them feeling more rather than less powerful, while respecting the need for external scrutiny of professional practice and, ultimately, the sanction of failure to license for practice? It is important that the programme's teaching on values such as empowerment are reflected in the way those values are assessed. In this way, individuals will be encouraged to learn from the process rather than to approach it defensively.

INVOLVING ALL STAKEHOLDERS

A holistic approach to learning and assessment is one which can encompass both competence and context. It is one which celebrates the diversity of perspectives of good practice and takes positive action to ensure that those who are less powerful are included in the process. Methods of assessment need to be found which are capable of reflecting this variety and which include those who have a stake in the outcome. This will create a climate in which assessors and assessed, together, can learn from the process of assessment.

Factors

If these principles are important for the system of assessment as a whole, let us look now at the factors which are specific to the portfolio itself, when seeking to integrate learning and assessment.

PROVIDING A STRUCTURE

To what extent should the responsibility for structuring the presentation lie with the individual learners or the assessors? Taylor *et al.* (1999, p.156) suggest that 'presenting material in a clear and concise fashion...should be part of the explicit assessment criteria for portfolios'. On the one hand is the fear that standardization will cramp the individual's style; on the other is the learner's own anxiety about not knowing what is expected, and their obsession with the mechanics of portfolios. At its extreme, this anxiety has led to a candidate submitting three lever-arch files of material for assessment.

Although the experience of constructing one's own assessment structure could be a learning experience, for many it is daunting; more an unwanted task than a liberation. There may be one or two learners who are itching to present their evidence in the form of a play or an extended poem, but the paradox is that giving learners a structure for the portfolio is likely to encourage rather than constrain innovation, in the way that having agreed rules and a ready-made board and pieces unleashes rather than inhibits the creativity of chess players.

The portfolio should, then, be structured as required by the assessors, but the structure must not be so constraining that learners are unable to speak with their own voice, nor should they look so smart that learners are 'apprehensive about writing in them for fear of making them look untidy' (Hull and Redfern 1996, p.9).

AN INVITATION TO A DIALOGUE

If the portfolio is to be an instrument of both learning and assessment, it needs to be construed as an invitation to a dialogue. It is a discussion which the learner has with him- or herself, a kind of reflective soliloquy. In common with a soliloquy, we all know that this dialogue with oneself, though seemingly private, is held before an audience. It is not just the content which is important, but also the quality of the dialogue as a dialogue. In other words, the assessor looks not just for evidence of specific accomplishments, but also for signs of the author's ability to question and maintain a continuing 'reflective dialogue' (Taylor *et al.* 1999, p.154).

It follows, therefore, that a portfolio that is seeking to integrate learning and assessment benefits from being structured around open questions, which lead the learner on to further questions rather than definitive answers.

FRAMING AND REFRAMING THE QUESTIONS

It is important that assessors, as well as the individual learners, demonstrate a commitment to dialogue, taking care to frame questions so that they encourage rather than inhibit reflective dialogue. We have examples from practice of the significance of framing questions, such as the 'change talk' of brief, solution-focused therapy:

> It is essential that the therapist create a language…from which pictures of changes can be drawn. So, the therapist asks, '*What* changes have happened since I last saw you?' rather than '*Have* any changes…' and '*When* things are better…' rather than 'If things get better'.
>
> (George, Iveson and Ratner 1990, p.7)

The assessors will demonstrate their own commitment to learning by continually responding to the experiences of authors of portfolios. Which questions are the most facilitative? How might others be changed? For assessors as well as assessed, the portfolio should be a work in progress.

TOTEM's dilemma

We will see what this means in practice shortly. First, let us return to TOTEM, the Training Organization for Tea-Making, where there are two warring factions. One faction strongly advocates partializing the assessment and using a competency approach, and has devised a list of learning objectives, which include:

- evaluate the appropriate lactic input
- determine levels of sucrosity
- ascertain the range of temperature variables
- substantiate environmental and utensil-related factors
- analyse the gustatory preferences of drinker-users
- reflect on the occupancy rates within the container.

The other faction is totally opposed and wants candidates to be given *carte blanche* to present evidence of their abilities as they wish. They call their approach holistic. However, as we know from our earlier analysis, this is a misunderstanding, since partializing is a necessary aspect of assessing professional practice in a holistic way. However, if this is divorced from context, the result is likely to be a language of assessment similar to the caricature above. The first steps towards a holistic approach would be to begin to frame these indicators as open questions. Perhaps the following italicized examples would encourage a discursive, questioning style:

- evaluate the appropriate lactic input

  How much milk did you put in, if any, and when did you add it?

- determine the levels of sucrosity

  Did you add sugar? If so, when and why?

- ascertain the range of temperature variables

  How did you find out how hot to serve the tea?

- substantiate environmental and utensil-related factors

  How important was the quality of the crockery? When you next make tea how will you decide what to serve it in?

- analyse the gustatory preferences of drinker-users

  What kinds of tea do people like? How and why does this vary?

- Reflect on the occupancy rates within the container

  Why is it important to consider the length of time the tea is brewing?

The adapted style does not use mystifying or pseudo-scientific language, being closer to the way we think and speak. Sadly, there is a tendency to associate plain language with lack of expertise and professionalism, whereas precisely the opposite is true. An idea expressed simply is not necessarily a simple idea. The challenge is to express complex ideas and situations in language which is as accessible and as direct as possible without, of course, doing any injustice to the original complexities.

We also notice that injunctions have been replaced by interrogatives, leading to open questions which, nevertheless, guide the learner towards focused responses. The one closed question, *Did you add sugar?* is followed by an open one. These are competencies in context. Although these particular questions remain focused on intrinsic qualities, their openness begins to invite the learner to contextualize this and reflect on them. Further questions could be asked to usher the learner towards contextual issues and invite consideration of the broader cultural relevance.

Signposting the portfolio

In order to put these principles and practices into operation, we have developed a portfolio system which provides 'signage' for the learner (Doel and Sawdon 1995, 1999a, 1999b). The signage is designed to integrate the processes of learning and assessment and goes beyond general guidance available to people who are compiling portfolios (Doel and Shardlow 1995). The signage is intended to help learners to articulate the tacit knowledge which their reflection draws on. It is written in direct language, in a discursive style, to encourage learners not just to answer questions but to ask further questions of themselves. The signage itself is a work in progress, since all of the questions can be improved.

One of the challenges facing the signposted portfolio as a tool of learning and assessment is how to provide a structure which is common and generic, and yet responsive to each individual learner. This is similar to road signage, where the planner must prioritize the most likely destination points and assume the traveller's knowledge of certain conventions, such as the road numbering system, symbols, colour coding, etc. New technology may soon enable individual travellers to find the precise information they want from each panel; in a similar way, this kind of technological advance may also allow each learner to have access to a tailored assessment structure. In the meantime, the signposted portfolio must cater to a mass market and hope to refine its questions in ways which are encompassing enough to house all learners, but not so broad as to be vacuous.

Organizing principles

The signposted portfolio has three organizing principles. The most self-evident is content. The overall content is divided (i.e. partialized) into sections and subsections of learning and assessment, which themselves mirror aspects of practice and curriculum content. Using 'Skills in Groupwork' as an example, 'Offering Groupwork' is an element of groupwork practice to be learned and practised; it forms a session in the groupwork training programme and it comprises a module for assessment in the groupwork portfolio (see Part 2, Section 3.1).

The portfolio is organized along another dimension, designed to help learners to process this content. Within each subsection of the portfolio, a series of questions prompts the learner to present and consider relevant evidence of learning and practice. The dialogue we explored earlier takes place through this constructive questioning, which signs the way for the learner. The questions are framed and grouped to trigger responses of the three kinds we outlined at the start of this chapter:

- *description* of the experience which is being presented as evidence, to encourage and test observation

- *analysis* of the experience, to encourage and test evaluative, subjective commentary and the wider context

- *reflection* on the experience, to encourage learners to 'helicopter' above it, testing their ability to see it from different perspectives and deliberate on their own learning.

The boundaries between description, analysis and reflection are not sharp, but learners have been able to make good use of the distinction (in effect, a partialization) to provide, ultimately, a better integrated practice. Within the questions, learners can also find the criteria by which their learning and practice will be assessed. The relationship between description, analysis and reflection has some parallels with the relationship we explored earlier between partial, contextual and holistic approaches to learning and assessment.

Anti-oppressive practice provides another organizing principle. It figures as a specific subdivision of the content, but it is also an element throughout the portfolio, by means of a regular bulletin to consider issues of power and oppression. The responses to the signpost questions should provide evidence of empowering practice and learning, but the learner is asked to name this learning and to develop a routine of reflecting on specific issues of power and oppression.

We hope that the signposted portfolio contests Velde's (1999, p.438) opinion that 'although research attempts are being made to explore more holistic conceptions of competence, these appear, in the main, not to be applied to actual practice'. The signposted portfolio is regularly providing practical evidence of the integration of partial and contextual approaches, to the benefit of both learning and assessment. Signposting provides the 'special help' which Walker (1985, p.62) notes some learners require to complete a portfolio. We think this special help is important for all learners.

Moving on

In their helpful article on portfolios for learning and assessment, Taylor *et al.* (1999) recommend the availability of exemplars to prepare panels of assessors. Exemplars are an essential aid for learners as well, so they can develop an image of what a portfolio looks like. Indeed, Schön's (1995) belief that practitioners' theory is actually revealed and transmitted through practice exemplars, not explicit 'espoused theory' or formal research findings, suggests that portfolios might be a significant way in which practitioners can make semi-formal accounts of their practice more widely available.

In Part 2 we reproduce a whole portfolio, successfully completed for credits towards the post-qualifying award in social work. It is presented not as a perfect example, but as an illustration of the way in which a practitioner can use a signposted portfolio to demonstrate learning as well as accomplishment in an area of social work practice. Although the content is specific to groupwork, and the groupwork specific to people with memory problems, we hope that Part 1 has helped prepare you for the general and universal issues which this specific example depicts.

So, we take the unusual step of reproducing a whole portfolio in the spirit of this oft-quoted Chinese proverb:

Tell me and I forget.
Teach me and I remember.
Show me and I understand.

PART 2

A signposted portfolio

Section 1
Introduction to the Portfolio

[The appendix and questionnaires were included in the original portfolio but have not been included in this book. Names have been changed.]

1.1 Context

Please give a brief description of who you are, where you work and the kind of work that you do. What has been your past experience of groups (as a member or a leader)? Also, give a brief pen picture of any co-leader(s).

My name is Diane Morrison and I am a social worker in a Community Mental Health Team (CMHT) for older persons. I am one of the two social workers in the team; the rest of the team consists of three community psychiatric nurses (CPNs), one full-time mental health support worker, and two part-time mental health support workers. Although we are supervized by a clinical nurse manager and a social work manager, neither is based with the team. This means we work very much on our own initiative.

I have been qualified for just over a year and have experienced a very steep learning curve – the challenge of working so much on my own has been exhilarating and, at times, frightening. The majority of my work is to assess need and coordinate care plans for people aged 65 and over who suffer from severe and enduring mental health problems (around two thirds suffer from a form of dementia). The aim is that individuals are supported to remain in their own homes (if this is their choice) for as long as possible.

Social work in such a setting offers few opportunities to practise groupwork, and I had little previous experience of facilitating a group. As a student on placement, in a CMHT for 18–65-year-olds, I co-facilitated a women's group, but did not contribute much to the planning.

I leapt at the chance to set up a group in my current job as there has always seemed to be a dearth of appropriate needs-led services in our area of Townham District. Rather unusually, I had not one, but three co-workers. This was because we felt we needed more staff to support the group in various activities.

My co-workers:

June T. is a mental health support worker who has been with the CMHT since its inception. Prior to that, she worked in a residential home for older people, and has practical experience of groupwork/activity work with older people. I have tended to look to June for ideas as I feel she is more experienced in this kind of work.

Bella R. is a social worker in the CMHT. She has always been enthusiastic about meeting the gap in service provision through groupwork, and was instrumental in finding funds for the group. Bella's previous experience of groupwork is similar to mine, and we have supported each other.

Wanda H. is a mental health support worker in the CMHT. Wanda works 16 hours a week and has given much more time to planning and running the group, showing her commitment and determination to make it a success. Wanda tended to look to Bella and myself for ideas and guidance at first, seeing us as the 'qualified workers'. I feel Wanda now has much more confidence in her own abilities as a groupworker, recognizing that her strengths and contributions are of equal importance.

The four of us work comfortably together, although we initially had varying expectations of our own roles and of the group's purpose.

1.2 The group project

Details of the Group being used to illustrate this portfolio.
Include a copy of your Group's Profile sheet below.

NAME OF THE GROUP: *Memory Joggers*

MAIN PURPOSE OF THE GROUP:

This is a group for people with memory problems who live in the Handley area.

The main aims are:

- to maintain, promote and encourage independence
- to provide social contact and stimulation
- to provide a quality service to a group of people whose needs are currently not met in the local area.

GROUP MEMBERSHIP:

Open or closed membership? The membership is open but relatively settled, and while people are encouraged to attend, no one is obliged to come. It is not a 'drop-in', as this would be unsettling for the regular attenders.

Number of members: 11

Largest group attendance	*Smallest attendance*	*Average attendance*
11	6	8

Age range of group members: From late 40s to late 70s

Gender and ethnic composition: All group members are white – this is representative of the over-65 population in Handley. There are two men in the group – the other members, including the groupworkers, are female.

Voluntary or compulsory membership: The group is voluntary, but as groupworkers, we recognize that some members may feel under pressure to attend.

GROUP SESSIONS:

Where did/does the group meet? The group initially met at Handley Health Centre, in the waiting room, which we 'set up' before the group began. Although the group met there for three sessions, we were forced to move because the Health Centre closed down. Our office moved to a previously closed ward at Northington Hospital, and we found a room which could be used solely for groupwork.

How often? The group meets every Monday afternoon.

How many sessions has the group had? The group has had over 20 sessions and is still going strong!

How long is each session approximately? Two hours, from approx. 2pm–4pm.

Open-ended or time-limited? We hope the group will continue, but Bella and I may not be able to remain as fully involved, once the groupwork training course is over, due to work demands and other pressures from our managers.

1.3 Pen pictures of group members

Give a brief description of each of the members of the group. Included in the pen picture should be the person's name (anonymized), age, gender and race; why they come to the group and what they hope to get from it; how regularly they attend; a brief description of how they are seen in the group ('good sense of humour', 'tends to wander off the point', etc.) You will be making reference to these individuals through-out the portfolio. Make sure names have been changed.

Grace is in her late 70s, is widowed and lives in sheltered accommodation. She acknowledges that she is having problems with her memory. She comes to the group for stimulation and company, because she enjoys being with other people and wants to retain her skills by sharing strategies of coping. Grace is a fairly dominant group member who initiates conversation and puts others at their ease. She is lively and enjoys a joke, feeling comfortable enough to talk in the large group and on a one-to-one basis. She attends every week.

Hannah is in her late 60s, widowed, and lives alone in a bungalow. Hannah is aware of the limitations of her memory and needs stimulation and company to prevent depression. Hannah participates well in the group, but needs encouragement to try other activities. The group is an event for her; she makes a big effort with her appearance and is always ready to be picked up. Hannah refuses to attend the other day services and initially came to the group because I would be there. (I am her social worker.) Hannah shares her ways of coping with the group and is very much an 'anchor' in the group. She has a good sense of humour and usually sits with Grace.

Peter is in his 70s and was referred by his social worker in South Empton Community Team – he lives alone and receives support from a community carer. He initially came to the group with the community carer, as he was nervous about attending, but she left him to it after about half an hour. He comes for the company, and has said he enjoys what we do. Peter is in his 70s, is very hard-of-hearing, and has short- and long-term memory problems, perhaps more than we initially thought. He is a quiet member who sits back and observes. He will do what he feels comfortable with, and perhaps needs more encouragement to try other activities. He is always ready when we pick him up, and attends every week.

Amanda is in her late 70s and lives with her husband in a flat. She has only recently moved to the area. Amanda had a tendency to forget that she was coming at the start of the group's life, but now she enjoys attending. Amanda is reluctant to acknowledge that she has memory problems when she talks to me on her own, but is more accepting of this in a group situation. She is good in the long-term memory games and finds it easier with prompt cards. Amanda keeps herself to herself, but is friendly when approached. She seems more comfortable with the groupworkers than other members. Amanda attends because she wants stimulation and the structure of the group seems to provide this for her – she responds to that. Amanda was referred by Bella.

Gillian has only attended the group on two occasions. She is in her mid-70s and lives with her grandson. She has mild memory problems and it has been uncertain whether these are caused by an organic or by a functional mental health problem. Gillian attends Day Treatment Services as well as coming to the group, and she has a multitude of physical health problems which have prevented her from attending the group.

Jane is in her 70s, lives with her two sons and is recently widowed. Jane experiences ongoing anxiety and depression and was recently diagnosed as having dementia. She sees the group as a chance to express herself, as she is stifled at home and wants to address her memory problems. Jane feels she is a burden and has low self-esteem – she wants to be liked and to feel she belongs. Jane is keen on art therapy and enjoys reminiscence activities; although she is quite dominant, her use of long-term memory prompts other group members.

Fred is in his 70s and was referred by his social worker in Handley Community Team, but subsequently referred to the CMHT. Fred experiences long- and short-term memory problems and can be unpredictable in mood. Sometimes he acts the clown and at other times he is very moody. On a 'good day' Fred has an excellent rapport with the groupworkers and members, and is viewed by the other members as a bit of a comic. He is an ex-boxer and a big man, and this could make him appear quite threatening; however, he is accepted by the others and well-liked. Fred can misinterpret situations and we need to be very focused in discussions as he can go off on tangents. Fred was a regular attender but then, after seven sessions, chose not to come any more.

Jenny is in her late 40s and lives with her husband and one of her sons. Jenny has Huntington's chorea, an early onset dementia. She was initially shy and reserved, observing but reluctant to speak in the group. Jenny was dependent on June, her support worker, at first, but is gaining in confidence. She does not volunteer information often, but will participate when prompted. Jenny needs one-to-one support in activities, and is viewed quite sympathetically by group members. She was encouraged to attend because it was felt she would benefit from the company and stimulation, and also because she will not attend other day services and her husband needs the break. Although quiet, Jenny talks about 'our' group – she sees herself as a group member.

Lily is in her late 60s and lives with her husband. She attends the group to get her out of the house, build on her confidence and to retain her skills. Lily has problems with her long- and short-term memory, coupled with poor coordination and impaired perception. As such, she often needs one-to-one support in the group. Lily is seen as a comic by other group members, and is a valuable member of the group as she will try any activity and is more adventurous in her ideas than the others. Lily will 'open up' more in smaller groupings where she finds support and draws strength from the others. Lily enjoys the stimulation and the identity of the group where, I suspect, she does not feel stigmatized.

Rita is in her 70s and lives at home with her son. She joined the group a few months after its inception and has become an important group member. She has long- and short-term memory problems which she finds very distressing at home, but in the group situation she calms down, acknowledging her problems and searching for ways of dealing with them. Rita is very matter-of-fact and the other group members respond well to this.

1.4 The relevant literature

You will be making reference to the general groupwork literature in the rest of the portfolio. On this page you need to reference any particular literature (policy documents, articles, chapters, books, etc.) relevant to the client group who are the members of your group. For example, if the group aims to bring together older, isolated people in the community, what have you learned by reading what has already been written about groupwork with this particular client group? You can give a brief outline of any references which are particularly significant.

Benson, J. (1987) *Working More Creatively with Groups.* London: Tavistock.

Bernard, L., Burton, J., Kyne, P. and Simon, J. (1988) 'Groups for older people in residential and day care: the other groupworkers.' *Groupwork 1*, 2, 115–123.

Bertcher, H. (1994) *Group Participation* (2nd edition). London: Sage.

Brown, A. (1992) *Groupwork*, (3rd edition). Aldershot: Arena.

Crimmens, P. (1998) *Storymaking and Creative Groupwork – Groupwork with Older People.* London: Jessica Kingsley Publishers.

Doel, M. and Sawdon, C. (1999) *The Essential Groupworker: Teaching and Learning Creative Groupwork.* London: Jessica Kingsley Publishers.

Douglas, T. (1978) *Basic Groupwork.* London: Tavistock.

Goffman, E. (1967) 'Nancy Deviants'. In T. Scheff (ed.) *Mental Illness and Social Processes.* New York and London: Harper and Row.

Heap, K. (1985) *The Practice of Social Work with Groups.* London: George Allen and Unwin.

Hodge, J. (1985) *Planning For Co-Leadership.* Newcastle: Tyne Ltd.

Mullender, A. (1990) 'Groupwork in residential settings for elderly people'. *Groupwork 3*, 3, 286–301.

Mullender, A. and Ward, D. (1989) 'Challenging familiar assumptions: preparing for and initiating a self-directed group.' *Groupwork* 2,1, 5–26.

Rice, S. and Goodman, C. (1992) 'Support groups for older people – is homogeneity or heterogeneity the answer?' *Groupwork* 5, 2, 65–77.

Shulman, L. (1984) *The Skills of Helping Individuals and Groups*. Illinois: FE Peacock.

Whitaker, D. (2000) *Using Groups to Help People* (2nd edition). London: Routledge.

Section 2

Planning the Group

2.1 Planning

Description

Please give a brief outline of the purpose and aims of the group. What did you do in order to plan for this group? For example, how did you find out about the need for this kind of group? What criteria did you use for membership? What practical details did you work on – venue, transport, etc?

AIMS AND PURPOSE OF *MEMORY JOGGERS*

- to help individuals maintain skills through physical and mental activities
- to empower individuals to take more control of their situations through structured discussion about memory problems and coping strategies
- to provide a safe forum where individuals can build on confidence and self-esteem with support from other group members
- to stimulate both short-term and long-term memories through reminiscence sessions and concentration exercises
- to enable individuals to widen their social contacts and networks through meeting with others in similar situations
- to ensure individuals have fun in a relaxed, informal environment.

When I started this job a year ago, Bella told me that it would be helpful to have two social workers in the team, as we could possibly provide our own service – a group of some kind. At this stage, we did not know what kind of group we wanted to run, and had done no real research into what was needed. There was a general awareness that there was not enough choice in the services for people over 65 with mental health problems in Handley town and the surrounding villages.

Over the next few months, Wanda joined the team, and expressed an interest in starting up a group with June – possibly for people experiencing anxiety and depression. At team meetings, we discussed the possibility and practicality of setting up our own service, asking ourselves questions such as, who would be involved, who would come, and did we have the time? The opportunity to participate in the 'Skills in Groupwork' training course was a catalyst to action.

After discussion with team members, staff at Beardsmore Resource Centre (the social services day centre for over-65s in our area) and staff at The Pinewoods (the health trust community unit for people with severe dementia and challenging behaviours), we recognized that there was a gap in service provision. All of us could identify service users who suffer from moderate memory problems and continue to live at home. The environment of Beardsmore is not always stimulating or structured enough for these people to maintain skills, and they do not always receive one-to-one attention, because it isn't practical with too many service users and too few staff. Beardsmore is not a specific service for people with memory problems. The Pinewoods, on the other hand, is a more specialist service, and many of our service users do not suffer from more advanced memory problems – they would feel stigmatized in such an environment and would not wish to stay. We decided to fill the gap in service provision with a service for people with moderate memory problems who do not fit the criteria for the two other day services available in our area.

CRITERIA

A group for people with moderate memory problems who live in the Handley area. It is a mixed-sex group.

VENUE

Following two course workshops and a consultation with the tutors, the four of us met to discuss the practicalities of running such a group. We had decided to use our own work base as a venue; it is a health centre, local to the area and close to Beardsmore, whose facilities we had been told we could use. Also, the clinic was rarely used. We decided to hold the group on Monday afternoons, when there was no surgery and no one else was in the building except the CMHT.

We discussed which room to hold the group in; initially, two rooms were possible. We eventually decided to use the main waiting room as it had a high ceiling, was lighter and was more roomy. We recognized we would have to move furniture around to prepare for the group, and also that the waiting room chairs were uncomfortable. Fortunately, we were able to order some 'Shackleton-style' chairs from social services stores – and got eight for free. There was a large poster screen in the waiting room which we planned to borrow, and the room was large enough to divide into sections for various activities, thus offering more choice (we hoped!) to the group members.

TRANSPORT

As there were four of us, we felt we could use our own cars to pick up group members and take them home.

REFERRALS

We had seven initial referrals from our own team, and we sent a poster (included as an Appendix in the actual portfolio) to the two local community teams, advertising the group. We eventually received a referral from each team.

GROUP CONTENT

As we were providing a day-centre-type service, we wanted the group to be 'activity-based'. We spoke to the staff at Townham Outreach to get ideas about running groups, e.g. games, exercises, crafts, etc. and they said they would send us some information. Both June and Wanda have worked with Outreach in the past. Bella and I spoke to staff at Day Treatment

Services, the day hospital in Churchland, and to Nancy, the activities organiser at Beardsmore. Both were very helpful giving us ideas about crafts, reminiscence exercises and relaxation tapes, and they offered us the use of their equipment (e.g. bingo machine, quiz sheets).

FINANCES

Our manager was supportive by providing £100 from the Care Programme Approach Budget in order to buy materials. We also planned to generate our own money for the group through raffles and charging for tea and coffee. In fact, we charged 10p for as much tea and coffee as group members wanted, and 5p for biscuits. Raffle tickets were 5p each and the proceeds financed raffle prizes and the Christmas meal.

We hoped to enlist the help of the CPNs and the occupational therapist at Churchland, particularly with anxiety management sessions and crafts. We were determined to highlight group member choice, and although we planned the first session, we intended to ask group members what they would like to do and plan the future sessions together.

Analysis

Why did you think there was a need for a group with these members at this time? What went well in the planning phase, and what was problematic?

As described in the previous section, there has always been a need for a group with these members. Handley, although part of Townham district, is on the outskirts, and older people with memory problems in our area do not have the same choice of appropriate day services as those living nearer to or in Townham. For example, Townham Outreach runs groups for older people with memory problems but their service does not extend to the Handley area. All four of us involved in planning the group could identify service users who attended Beardsmore but who needed more structured support from a day service.

In a sense, *Memory Joggers* was initially tailored specifically to meet the needs of these people, and with particular service users in mind, we focused on what *they* needed from a group. I think this helped us in the planning process, because we had specific individuals in mind when discussing our aims and purposes, and so we were clearer about what we were setting out to achieve. Brown (1992, p.8) points out that groupwork, like social work, began by focusing on helping the individual with a problem; however, he goes on to say that 'contemporary groupwork emphasises action and influence as well as reaction and adaptation'. At the planning phase, however, we were concerned with individual need and how to meet this via a group experience. Our reasoning behind this is described by Douglas (1978, p.63); 'many people believe that their particular problem is absolutely unique to them, and they frequently get a great deal of support when they are placed in a situation where they realise that this is not true and they are not alone'.

I feel the planning phase was quite successful, in that we had received promises of support and these were honoured by staff at Day Treatment Services and Nancy, the activities organizer at Beardsmore. We successfully applied for money from the Care Programme Budget, and received initial funds for tea/coffee/biscuits from the Health Trust. The four of us had a lot of motivation and enthusiasm at the planning phase, and we felt our group was supported by the team and by our manager.

We did not experience any problems in identifying potential members, mainly because the group was shaped around them rather than being conceived first and then searching for people to fit the criteria. This way we could be sure we were really meeting people's needs. We were also pleased by the response we got from the community teams; two referrals and much interest in the group's development.

When we mentioned the idea to service users, relatives and carers, they were enthusiastic and some even donated raffle prizes! We felt we had done the best we could with our choice of venue, and although we recognized that it was not ideal, we felt it would suffice.

On the flipside, we had some difficulties pinning down some people, such as the occupational therapist, who equivocated about her involvement, and eventually decided to set up her own group instead.

Reflection

What changes would you make if you were planning the same kind of group again? What have you learned about your groupwork practice at this stage in the work?

I initially thought I would not make any changes if planning the same kind of group again, as I felt we were very thorough. However, with hindsight, there would be some important changes. First, we never seriously considered the health and safety aspects of our group, and did not ask permission from the Health Trust to hold the group in their building. This oversight was highlighted on the day of the first session when we arrived at work to discover that we had been broken into and that the group room was unfit for use. Until then we had not even considered whether we were insured to hold a group in the building. If we had incorporated this into our planning phase, we would have eliminated the need for frantic phone calls and panics on the morning of the first session.

Next, we have encountered some hostility towards the group from certain team members, which was not apparent in the initial planning stage. We realized that all our discussions with the team about the group should have been minuted, and that circulating our aims and purposes in written form prior to starting the group would have saved confusion and bad feeling later on.

Also, with hindsight, we should not have named the group ourselves. Bella came up with the name *Memory Joggers*, which I still feel is catchy and appropriate. However, if we had allowed the group to choose, the act of choosing could have helped foster a sense of group identity: 'a very concrete way of helping the group to gain a sense of increasing control and responsibility for itself is to help it to find itself a name' (Doel and Sawdon 1999, p.59). Because we were new to groupwork and relatively unsure of ourselves, I think choosing the name gave us a degree of power and control. I do not think we would have been confident enough to initiate group choice of the name in the first session. In future, I would feel more confident in giving the group that choice.

Throughout the planning phases, I recognized the importance of making time. All the groupwork literature emphasizes how vital it is to set aside specific planning time with co-workers, and this is paramount. At the planning phase, we did manage to make time for meetings, and it is unfortunate that we did not manage our time quite so well later on. I have learned the importance of detailed planning, but also that groupworkers must be prepared to be flexible when something does not go to plan. For example, even though we planned well, we could not have anticipated that we would be broken into the night before the first session, and our plans had to be flexible enough to cope with the problems this caused.

2.2 Co-working in groups

Description

If you have been working with a partner, describe how you decided to work together and what you do to oil the wheels of the partnership. Give one or two specific examples from a group session to illustrate the partnership at work. If you have not had a co-worker, describe why this has been the case.

I have three co-workers in the *Memory Joggers* group. We decided to work together because we had all felt there was a need for this kind of group, and we had each mentioned that we would like to be involved in organizing a group. The divisions were initially apparent; as social workers, Bella and I had talked about the possibility of setting up a group, and separately, Wanda and June had discussed the need for a group for many of the isolated people they support in the community. When the opportunity arose to take part in the 'Skills in Groupwork' course, the four of us separately expressed interest and it was only then that Wanda told me she and June had been discussing the pros and cons of running a group, and I said Bella and I had been talking about it, too.

Initially, we were going to run separate groups. However, our manager suggested that the four of us could co-work, and this would allow cover for holidays and absences without having to cancel any of the sessions. The 'Skills in Groupwork' course tutors supported this suggestion, emphasizing that it would help us to learn from one another, too.

As we work in the same team, we see each other regularly, which aids our working relationships as we can see how the others cope within the work setting, and we have all seen each other stressed at work! We have also supported each other within the team, and I think this is reflected within the group; when one of us has had a hard day, the others compensate. (For example, when Wanda's car radiator flooded, she was stressed and had to leave the group halfway through and take it to a garage. Bella and I were able to reassure her that it was OK to do this. Perhaps even more important, the group members also supported Wanda that day.) We recognize that we each have different experiences and abilities, and this is often implicit in our groupwork together. For example, when planning, I look to June for ideas on crafts and artwork, and in a group session, I often use non-verbal communication with Wanda so she gives additional support to certain group members. We have become quite adept at picking up each others' signals and vibes, and acting on them accordingly, but it has taken time and commitment to reach this stage.

I give an early example of partnership at work in the Power and Oppression notes which follow this section (Section 2.3). A later example of our co-working shows how we each contributed to a session, seemingly individually, but working together to help the group find an identity for itself. In many sessions, one or two of us were absent, but in this particular session we were all there, which enabled us to offer a wider choice of activities to group members in the latter part of the session. Following our refreshments break, we each approached group members, asking them what they would like to do. June offered a craft-based activity (painting and varnishing flower-pots ready for seed-planting), Bella offered a games activity (dominoes, cards or Scrabble), Wanda offered one-to-one with a group member who had been feeling low in the earlier part of the session (they ended up doing a jigsaw together and chatting) and I offered support to the group members who wished to relax, observe others and socialize at a general level. Each of us was able to facilitate an activity, promoting choice and enabling participation, while implicitly restating the group's aim of stimulation through enjoyment and creativity. The use of specific action techniques to achieve this aim was helped by us being clear about our goals for the group, and responsive to the goals of individual members. We are much more aware now, having co-worked, that we can use our different skills to work towards the same aim.

Analysis

How did you evaluate how effective these co-working arrangements were? If you did not have a co-worker, what differences do you think it would have made to the group if you had had a partner?

Many groupwork theorists expound the advantages of co-working and use the term carefully, as opposed to co-leading (Hodge 1985). There was initially a hierarchy of leadership in our co-working relationship, as June and Wanda perceived Bella and me to be more capable of 'leading' the group. Brown (1992) discusses power and leadership, and this has helped me to recognize that, through my own anxieties and inexperience in groupwork, I started out by assuming the leader role, which was also partly thrust on me by my co-workers. I was not comfortable with this role because it felt unequal. Brown (1992, p.74) writes, 'if the worker has not come to terms with her own power and authority, she is unlikely to be able to help the members discover and use theirs'. I was able to discuss my uncomfortable feelings with my co-workers, and gradually, as our confidence grew, the co-working relationship became more equal.

Co-working in groups has advantages for both workers and members (Brown 1992; Hodge 1985). For the group members, it offers diversity – the four of us have different personalities, styles of working, experiences and ideas. If a group member feels unable to relate to one of us at a particular time, it is likely that they can relate to one of the other groupworkers. For us, benefits include mutual support, both within and outside of the group, and professional development. We have been able to learn from each other and I have valued the abilities of my co-workers to tune in to the feelings of the group when I have been the main facilitator during an activity. In a group like ours it has been especially important to have several workers as there are group members who need one-to-one support during the group itself. We have noticed that these group members participate less when one or two of us are absent from the group.

Reflection

What would you keep and what would you change if you and your co-leader(s) were to work together again? If you did not have a co-worker, what impact did this have on you?

Initially we had different ideas about what we wanted to achieve in the group, even though we had already agreed on our aims and purposes. I think Wanda and June felt more relaxed about the group members just enjoying themselves, even if it meant playing three games of bingo and doing little else in a session. Bella and I, on the other hand, felt group members needed to be more challenged in the sessions, in order to justify the purpose of the group, and stop it from becoming a 'tea-party'. I think it was easy to lose sight of what the group members themselves actually wanted, and, having discussed this as a group, we are now agreed on the current structure of the session, which does include bingo and memory games.

Shared values are important amongst co-workers (or, at least, sharing what your values are). If we were to start the planning phase from new, I would have used something like the Sentence Completion exercise (Doel and Sawdon 1999, pp.214–215) to look at specific potential sticky moments in a group to see how we would each respond. For example, 'If a group member spent the whole session in silence, I would…'.

I am confirmed in my view that a group like *Memory Joggers* does benefit from (perhaps requires?) four workers to meet fully the needs of the group members. I recognize that we four constitute a 'group' and I am only just beginning to relate my learning about groupwork processes with *Memory Joggers* to group processes amongst our leadership group. It would be interesting to work in a group with just one other worker to experience the differences. I have had a taste of this when there has been only me and either Wanda, June or Bella in the group. We need to define our roles in each session more clearly in order to avoid too much overlap or confusion.

I would like us to have more time to reflect on our session, and to plan other sessions; this has been a cause of anxiety to all of us, because the logistics of the four of us setting aside planning time each week have been nightmarish. The sessions which have been planned by the four of us have been noticeably better for workers and members alike, as opposed to the sessions cobbled together at the last minute by one or two of us. This was evident in the groupwork logs, supplied by the 'Skills in Groupwork' training programme. We used these logs to record and evaluate the group.

As co-workers, I think we need to evaluate our own groupwork more rigorously, checking out with each other the impact of various action techniques and employing those which, after analysis, are the most effective. If the group has been successful so far, why is that? What is it about our use of groupwork skills which makes groupwork valuable for this service user group?

2.3 The planning phase: issues of power and oppression

For us, planning highlighted many dilemmas about the content of our groupwork and the make-up of the group. We assumed the group would be a positive experience, bringing together isolated people with the same kinds of problems. However, such a group can also 'amplify any existing sense of exclusion' (Doel and Sawdon 1999, p.50). In an article describing four different groups for older people, Bernard *et al.* (1988) illustrate this in a 'Memory Diary' group for people with severe dementia, in which one lady felt disempowered and distressed by the association of herself with others who had memory problems. We decided, therefore, not to focus too heavily on the issue of memory problems at first, instead emphasizing the fun and social nature of the group.

I was aware of what Brown (1992, p.38) calls the 'power of institutional forces', that running a group in the community holds less stigma than running it in a hospital. However, the irony is that we were forced to move the group when the health centre closed and the CMHT moved to a disused ward on Northington Hospital. The group came with us. In fact, the group room in the hospital is much more pleasant than the waiting room at the clinic, but the hospital setting could imply a medicalized approach. Through the group, we wanted to move away from 'the medical model of caring for a person's physical needs towards a more holistic and person-centred approach' (Crimmens 1998 p.15).

We faced a major dilemma when considering the 'mix' of group members and the question of gender. We toyed with the idea of a women-only group; 'women meeting in groups provide a source of strength through shared experiences, and a potential increase in control over their own lives, whether as members of the community or the agency' (Brown 1992, p.158). We did not know whether women would feel able to talk freely if there were men present; or feel overshadowed, especially as older women who have lived in a patriarchal society. Conversely, if the group was mixed, would the men feel marginalized, particularly as we, as groupworkers, were four women? In an article on support groups for older people, Rice and Goodman (1992, p.66) discuss how to 'balance the diversity of resources offered by heterogeneity against the enhanced intimacy or cohesiveness offered by homogeneity'. On balance, we felt that a mixed group would better represent the nature of our work and society as a whole; in a women-only group, would the implied message be that only women experience memory problems? We knew there could be potential difficulties in a mixed group but hoped the benefits would outweigh the disadvantages. 'Integration and proximity builds understanding between people, whereas segregation promotes discrimination' (Rice and Goodman 1992, p.71).

Another issue was age. Our potential group members were aged between late 60s and late 80s, representing different generations. We also had a potential group member who suffers from early onset dementia and is in her late 40s. We needed to be sensitive to these differences in age when planning the sessions, and what impact this would have on the group. However, we hoped that the diversity of experiences would enrich the group rather than hinder it.

In the planning phase, we needed to be aware of the power that we, as groupworkers, held. I think we were all quite overburdened with the perceived power imbalance at first, and this related not just to worker–member relationships, but power within the leadership group, too. I will illustrate this with an example of our co-working in the first session. Although we prepared the opening statement (see Section 3.3), and practised its presentation together, it was Bella and I who actually delivered it to the group. This highlights some of the initial power differences in our co-working relationship, and Wanda and June looked to Bella and me as the 'experienced' workers, when actually June has more experience than any of us in groupwork. We have been able to address this imbalance, both in consultation sessions with the course tutors, and in planning sessions.

The Early Stage

3.1 Offer to individuals

Description

How did you make the idea of the group known to potential group members? What three or four main points were you hoping to convey? Describe the offer of groupwork service to somebody who became a group member (and somebody who declined the groupwork service, if there is an example of this).

All four of the co-workers knew certain people we hoped would become group members and made the idea of groupwork known to potential members on our individual visits. We spoke about our ideas for the group and whether they felt it would be useful for them, prior to making a 'formal' offer of groupwork. We sent posters advertising the group to the two local community teams, so they could identify potential members from their service users, and make referrals to us. These posters were for social services staff to see, not service users. (An example was included in the original portfolio.) I contacted the Community Team Manager and he discussed the idea of the group at the team meeting, and our manager also promoted the group to the community team.

As groupworkers, we decided each of us would make the offer of groupwork to certain potential members. It seemed appropriate that, where the potential member was known to one of us, that person would make the offer. Our main points were that it was a group for older people with some memory problems, who were quite isolated, possibly without other services, to get together and enjoy themselves. It would be filling a gap in the kind of day services currently provided, was specifically for people in this area, and transport was provided.

OFFERING GROUPWORK TO HANNAH

I am Hannah's social worker, and felt that she would benefit from this kind of group. I raised the possibility of the group with Hannah, describing the main aims of the group and that it would be held on Monday afternoons. I said it would be a social group where Hannah could meet others, could take part in craft-based activities and would have a choice about what she wanted to do. I was tailoring the group to Hannah's interests in order to make it attractive to her, and so she knew what she could gain from attending. With Hannah's consent, I also discussed the group with her niece (Hannah's main carer). Hannah has been attending the group since its start.

OFFERING GROUPWORK TO MAVIS

The group had been running for over a month when I identified Mavis' need for such a service. I offered the group to Mavis in the same way as I had to Hannah, outlining the purposes of the group and the activities on offer, and also described a typical session to her. I emphasized how it could meet particular needs (in this case, easing isolation, developing coping strategies, dealing with anxiety). However, Mavis was reluctant to take up the offer of groupwork. Doel and Sawdon (1999, p.53) point out that 'group members may have internalized feelings of discrimination to the extent that they find it difficult to see themselves in an alternative light'. I feel this is also true of potential group members – Mavis feels marginalized in her life and is scared to face new challenges.

Analysis

Evaluate how you went about offering the idea of the group to individual members – how was this influenced by their circumstances (did they already know each other?)

We recognized that while we would be offering the group to different people, we needed a framework so that we all conveyed the same points. In some ways, we were making assumptions about what the potential group members' needs were, but these assumptions were based on assessments in which the service users participated. We also had to be aware that some potential group members would know each other, from other services or in general; however, we used this as a 'hook' and saw it as a positive aspect which would make the group seem less daunting. It was the idea of 'familiar faces'.

It is fortunate that we did not have to go to great lengths to attract people to the group, as we felt certain the need for this kind of group was real. Through our work, we also knew who we felt were the most appropriate potential group members, taking into account the level of memory difficulty, the mix of skill and ability, and the male–female dilemma described earlier. We asked the women and men separately their thoughts about a mixed group, bearing in mind that they might not necessarily tell us how they really felt, as older people are often less likely to question or complain.

We recognized the importance of downplaying our power and offering a choice to potential group members – we wanted to make it very clear that it was *their* group, and they should bring any ideas they had about the form they wanted the group to take. However 'choice' is relative and 'in some circumstances people may feel that to refuse groupwork might be detrimental to other aspects of the service they receive' (Doel and Sawdon 1999, p.105). This could have been true of our potential group members, as all bar two were known to one (or several) workers in the CMHT.

Reflection

With hindsight, how would you go about this differently next time?

With hindsight, I would have made our offer of groupwork more relaxed by asking potential members without their carers present. All the carers of potential members were very keen on the group, and although the group is voluntary, group members may have felt pressured or coerced to attend. This could have been due to feelings of wanting to please, guilt or the fear that 'refusal to comply could have adverse consequences or repercussions' (Brown 1992, p.32). We should make it very clear to potential group members that saying 'no' is a valid choice, and they are to be supported in that choice. Also, that the opportunity exists to say 'yes' at a later stage, if they wish (this is true of our group, as it has open membership).

I did not consider the possibility of 'exchanging'. In other words, how the dynamic would have changed if I had offered the groupwork service to, say, June's individual clients and she to mine. This might have helped potential members to see the groupwork service as an additional and different one; however, on balance, I think the safety of having someone they knew talk about the possible group was the right decision.

3.2 Tuning in skills

Description

What do you understand to be 'tuning in skills'? What were your feelings and thoughts before the first session of the group? What kinds of feelings and thoughts did you anticipate the group members had before the first session began?

Put at its most simple, 'tuning in' is an attempt to put yourself in the shoes of the group members to develop empathy for their likely situation (Shulman 1984, p.22). It is important to tune in to your own thoughts and feelings as a groupworker, too.

Before the first session, I was worried about the activities we hoped to do in the group, particularly the arts and crafts. I felt that none of us had the knowledge or expertise to run a session on crafts, even though we had plenty of materials, such as glass, paints and ceramics. In addition, despite our planning, I was very nervous that we had not planned enough! As a novice groupworker, I was anxious about my own abilities: would the group members feel that I did not have enough experience to lead such a group? I felt concerned that they would feel I was too young and could not empathize with their own experiences. At the same time, I was also very excited about the prospect of our planning actually coming to fruition, although this planning was tempered by the fact that we had been broken into, and until that lunchtime, we were unsure if we could even run the group, owing to fire regulations and the mess the intruders had left.

I had to be aware of group members' feelings and acknowledge that they would probably be different from my own. I needed to recognize that for most group members, the biggest effort was just being there. As a result of their age, their memory problems, and their isolation these were disempowered people. I anticipated that the group members would also be feeling quite nervous and unsure about what would happen in the first session. I had 'tuned in' to how individual members had responded when the offer of groupwork was made to them, and had realized that they felt nervous at the prospect of taking up a new challenge, such as meeting new people. What would be expected of them? Would they be 'tested'? Would they enjoy it?

As well as tuning in to how I felt a group of older people with memory problems were likely to feel in general (that is, marginalized, anxious and unimportant) while guarding against stereotypes, I practised tuning in to individual feelings. We knew most group members, so we were able to combine our knowledge of their circumstances to anticipate how they would be feeling. I knew Hannah and Grace experienced panic attacks and could guess they would be feeling anxious and nervous about the group. I knew that Lily was experiencing problems at home and felt her mind would not be on coming to the group.

Analysis

What did you do in response to your own thoughts and feelings before the first session, and those which you anticipated group members would have? How accurate do you think you were in anticipating group members' thoughts and feelings?

Of 'tuning in', Heap (1985, p.43) writes that 'so much that has been abstract is about to become reality; so much that has been speculation in the world of ideas and theory is about to be materialized in a group of troubled people'. Listening first to my 'feelings' rather than my 'thoughts' and being able to share this made me more ready to face the challenge of the group. Indeed, expressing and verbalizing my hopes and fears before the first session was liberating. I shared my feelings with Bella, June and Wanda, and discovered that while we were tuning in in similar ways, there were also specific differences. It was comforting to know that some of my worries were not shared by the others; for example, June was not concerned about the arts and crafts. Indeed, she felt fine about this, and it was a relief to know that at least one of us felt confident in this area. I realized how important it was to acknowledge my own feelings and thoughts: 'how you feel has a big impact on how you act. Tuning in to your own feelings lessens their power to block you' (Doel and Sawdon 1999, p.108).

Being able to tune in to members' probable feelings and how this informs their behaviour is useful in anticipating the outcome of group dynamics. However, Heap (1985) warns against following hunches too closely; this can lead to self-fulfilling prophecies. For example, I felt Fred would be a dominant member of the group, but needed to put this aside so I did not make assumptions about his actions.

At the start of the group session, it seemed that my anticipations of group members' feelings were reasonably accurate, and they were all fairly nervous and quiet at the start. However, by the end of the session, we checked out our assumptions with the group members and found that they seemed relieved that we had also been feeling anxious about the group, and were glad that it had gone so well.

Reflection

On reflection, do you think the prevailing feelings and thoughts changed as the group progressed? Evaluate how you tuned in to a later group session.

I think I 'tuned in' quite well to the potential group members before offering groupwork, since the majority of the potential group members became actual group members.

I know that for myself, my co-workers and most group members, the prevailing thoughts and feelings changed as the group progressed. As we became less anxious and more confident as group facilitators, so they became more confident and open as group members. The groupwork literature does refer to 'modelling' as a groupwork technique (Benson 1987; Doel and Sawdon 1999; Heap 1985) and although I was not consciously aware of it at the time, I now understand how this occurred. At a later session, Wanda and I were working with a group of just six members, and we checked our assumptions with them and with each other. We all felt comfortable enough to say that we enjoyed being part of a smaller group, without feeling disloyal to those not present, and felt more able to express our feelings. Indeed, in that particular session, we were able to focus more on members' fears of memory loss. We were able to learn from this discussion and when we had a larger group, we planned to split up into smaller groups for activities around memory problems.

An important aspect of tuning in is for the groupworkers to debrief when recording, after a session has ended. We found that we did not always have time to do this and I think that this did reflect negatively on our groupwork practice. It is easy to take for granted that you are tuned in to a group you know well, but their feelings (and your own) can change. When we did debrief after a session, the following one always seemed to run better.

3.3 Opening Statement of Purpose

Description

Briefly summarize your Opening Statement of Purpose. Give a brief summary of the first session of the group.

We decided that Bella and I would share the opening statement between us. Bella began by welcoming everyone to the group, and talking about the name of the group – *Memory Joggers*. She said that some of the group members would already know some of the groupworkers, but that we would introduce ourselves, and the four of us did so. Bella explained that we all had something in common – memory problems – and that we would be looking at ways of dealing with memory problems throughout the sessions of the group. I then explained to group members that we had some ideas for games and activities, but wanted to know about their ideas, as we wanted it to be a group based on what they wanted to do. I said that we had already planned the first session, in order for everyone to get to know each other. I said we would all begin by introducing ourselves, and talking a bit about what our first names mean to us, and then do some gentle exercise, to get everyone loosened up and moving. After this, the groupworkers would go round each member, offering a choice of three activities, such as dominoes and glass painting, and we would gather group members' ideas. Then, following a tea break and a raffle, we would get back together for a discussion. I closed by emphasizing that the most important thing about the session was to enjoy ourselves and have fun!

Analysis

Why did you decide on the particular features of your Opening Statement of Purpose, and how did you find out whether it 'worked'?

We planned our opening statement in one of the 'Skills in Groupwork' training workshops. We did not want to emphasize memory problems too heavily at the start, and we felt the tone of the opening statement should be informal and friendly, while still offering a structure. It seemed important to highlight that we were all together as a group because we were experiencing some problems with memory, in order to reinforce a sense of cohesiveness and belonging, but it did not seem appropriate to scare people off by discussing the implications of this in more detail.

An opening statement of purpose is an opportunity for groupworkers to present their ideas and purposes as negotiable material. The opening statement 'facilitates and encourages members in either identifying with them as their own aims or in supplementing and modifying them' (Heap 1985, p.44). By setting out a proposed structure for the first session, in a supportive and friendly manner, we hoped to make our aims and purposes clear, while still allowing for group members' choice. We made clear the point that we wanted group members to take part in the planning of other sessions by sharing their thoughts and ideas with us. We also hoped to make this seem less threatening by emphasizing that we would be speaking to each member individually about this.

We felt we did need a structured framework for the group sessions and the opening statement reminds group members of this structure, as well as providing safety and demonstrating that the group leaders intend to be actively involved and there (Whitaker 2000). We did not want to place too much pressure upon group members in their first session, but we did want to be clear that they had a choice of activities, and the opportunity to express their own ideas.

After the session, we debriefed and discussed whether we felt the opening statement had achieved our aims of ice-breaking, welcoming, offering choice and setting out our proposed structure in an informal manner. The opening statement was even more informal than we first thought, and group members kept chipping in as we were talking. This set the tone of the session and it was cheering that people felt comfortable enough to comment at this early stage.

Reflection

With hindsight, what specific changes would you make to the Opening Statement of Purpose? How do you feel the Opening Statement helped or hindered the rest of the first session?

The opening statement worked as an ice-breaker, but I have learnt that in every session we must make reference to our opening statement. Therefore, with hindsight, I would have shortened it, as we needed to make it more concise so that group members could identify with it more easily. Given the nature of their memory problems (short-term worse than long-term) most group members forget the purposes of the group each time they come. We have all found it useful to simplify our purposes; namely, we are meeting to share ways of dealing with memory problems and we do this through different kinds of activities. This has had the desired effect of some members realizing that they do come to the group for a reason other than to socialize. I have also been able to reflect that the stimulation gained from social contact is reason enough to come to the group, even though I do not feel tested as a 'skilled' groupworker.

I have already described the way in which the opening statement fell to Bella and me; with hindsight, I would now ensure that all four of us were involved if we were to do it again.

3.4 The early phase: issues of power and oppression

Offer to individuals

We were aware that some group members would know each other, and that this could create a power imbalance in the group before we began. The group members who did not know anyone could feel that the group was 'cliquey', and we really wanted everyone to start off on an equal footing.

We had to recognize the difference between choice and coercion. In other words, the factors which make people say 'yes' to groupwork can come from outside themselves, such as pressure from carers. Also, we had to consider how difference would be perceived by the group; for example, in Jenny's case, she was years younger than the other members. How might we best encourage group members to celebrate their differences?

Tuning In

It was important to understand that making assumptions about people can be dangerous, as people who have been made to feel powerless in other settings may see the group as a safe place to exercise power (for example, Jane and Fred as dominant members). It is a difficult balance between anticipating likely feelings and then looking for those feelings because you have been anticipating them.

Opening Statement

I recognized the importance of avoiding jargon which could reinforce group members' feelings of disempowerment. Even using the 'we' word can be tricky. Although it was true that '*we* would all be looking at ways of dealing with memory problems' it was not so true that '*we* all had something in common – memory problems'. It is uncomfortable using the word 'you' in those circumstances because it sets us (the groupworkers) aside.

Inevitably, we are exercising our professional power and this makes the relationship unequal. Professionals have the power to define the needs and problems of service users, rather then accept the service users' definitions. The group is a real opportunity for members to assert their own view of their situation and to gain power from each other to do this.

The Work Phase

4.1 Putting a session together

Description

Take one of your sessions and describe its structure and what happened in the session. (Choose any session but the first one, which you have already described in your Opening Statement of Purpose).

The session I am using to illustrate this section is Session 5.

We began the session as usual, by settling everyone into chairs, offering drinks and biscuits. Once everyone had finished their drinks and felt comfortable, I began by reiterating our Opening Statement of Purpose in condensed form. I said that we were all here because we were experiencing some problems with our memories, and that there were different ways of coping with this by focusing on stimulating different parts of our brains. I then introduced a 'name game', saying that this game stimulated short-term memory, while also stimulating the body through gentle exercise. Bella added that the exercise would also increase mental stimulation.

THE NAME GAME

We sat in a circle, I held the beanbag, said my name, and passed it to my neighbour, who said her name and passed it on, and so on. We did this three times. Then I held the beanbag, said someone's name, and threw the beanbag to that person. They had to catch it and throw it back to me, saying my name; we repeated this until everyone had thrown it back to me.

Finally, we had to pass the beanbag amongst ourselves, trying to remember each other's names. This generated discussion about short-term memory problems: how difficult it was to remember names, and ways of coping with this, such as remembering nicknames.

PROVERBS

Bella introduced the next game as a long-term memory stimulator. Wanda handed each of us a card, on which was written half a proverb or familiar phrase, like 'too many cooks…'. When everyone had a card, Bella invited each group member to read out and complete the phrase on their card. This prompted a lively discussion about proverbs and their meanings. As groupworkers, we took the opportunity to initiate discussion about the ease with which the group members remembered the proverbs, and that this was tapping into their long-term memory.

Following these games, we asked if group members would like a game of bingo, which is something they all said they enjoyed. We collected 20p from each of them; ten pence towards the cost of the prize and ten pence for drinks. June was the bingo caller and the winner chose a prize from our selection, typically smellies or chocolate.

After the bingo we made drinks for those who requested them, and invited them to engage in an activity of their choice; this week, the choices included painting and decorating flowerpots, doing a jigsaw, chatting, and playing cards or dominoes. Each group member was encouraged to choose an activity, and the groupworkers facilitated each activity.

As it neared 4pm we asked the members to move their chairs back into a circle so we could spend five minutes reflecting on the session, and we asked group members to talk about whether they had found specific parts of the session interesting or useful and whether they had enjoyed it. We also asked them if they could remember how we had started the session.

At 4pm, or thereabouts, we got ready to leave and transported people home.

Analysis

Comment on the degree of structure in the session you have described. What would be the advantages of having the session more structured or less structured? How did you and/or group members decide on the particular content of this session? How did you find out whether the session worked well?

This session was fairly structured, as we had planned it in some detail beforehand. As groupworkers, we had found from tuning in to a previous session that the group members felt comfortable with a structure, as they knew what to expect on arrival to a session. Some degree of structure and routine is less disorienting for people experiencing memory problems, even though the actual content of the sessions differed from week to week. We wanted to continue to highlight that one of the main aims of the group is to deal with memory problems, sharing experiences and breaking the taboo of memory loss. We hoped the memory games would be a positive experience for the group members, so we began with the 'harder' game, as this emphasized the poor short-term memory experienced by many group members. However, the group members turned this game into an enjoyable exercise, by throwing and dropping the bean bag, laughing at and with each other, and sometimes surprising each other by remembering names. Interestingly, we played this game again in a much later session, with a smaller group, and they were able to remember more names.

By having the 'Proverbs' game next, group members were encouraged to feel positive about their memories; they all had good recall for long-term memory and seemed empowered by this knowledge. Prompt cards helped to provide a reference point and focus on the task in hand. I feel that the first half of the session was very structured, and that this was an advantage for several reasons:

- The discussion on different ways of stimulating memory set the scene for focusing on short-term memory, followed by long-term memory.

- The group members were able to follow specific instructions which lessened the pressure on them to perform or provide what they felt would be the 'right' answer.

- By following the structure we were able to focus our discussions on particular issues, such as coping strategies for remembering names, embarrassment about forgetting names, sharing memories about proverb meanings, and acknowledging the differences in long- and short-term memory.

I think it would have been quite difficult for the group members if this part of the session had been less structured, as they would find it hard to begin games without clear guidance, and some members need quite a lot of support in this. If the games had been less structured, particularly without prompt cards, I think group members could have struggled to engage in the activity, and this could have been a negative experience for them.

The four of us planned the first part of the session, without input from group members. We chose the memory games from books we have on working with older people. From our experience of previous sessions, we learnt that some group members found it hard to contribute to games which involved general questions to the group as a whole, such as broad reminiscence or remembering things without prompts. This allowed the group to be dominated by a few members. However, with more structure, everyone could be involved. We also felt that if we began each session by restating our initial 'opening statement' from the very first session, then doing a game involving short-term memory followed by a game requiring exercise of long-term memory, the group members would feel secure in a remembrance of a pattern. Ideally, we would have liked group members to work with us in deciding the content of the games, but none of them has felt able to do this yet, although we always encourage it.

The second half of the session was deliberately less structured. The group members have chosen to play bingo each week. They find it non-stressful and relaxing, after the stimulation of the memory games. Bingo also generates money to buy prizes, tea and biscuits! Every member is able to play bingo (one or two need assistance) and it emphasizes the fun aspect of the group. For the final part of the session, the members decided on which activities to do from three or four on offer. We discovered that too much choice put group members on the spot, as they are not able to assimilate all the information. While we encouraged involvement in an activity, Hannah and Rita chose to sit outside, have a cigarette and chat. This choice was recognized as valid; socializing is a beneficial activity, especially for people who are usually isolated in their homes.

In the period of reflection at the end of the session, some group members were able to express their feeling more vocally than others. Overall, it was useful in 'grounding' the group members; some members found it difficult to remember what we had done at the beginning but, when prompted, said they had enjoyed it. It was also useful for us, as groupworkers, to evaluate the effectiveness of the content of the session.

Reflection

What would you keep and what would you change about the way you planned this particular session?

I would definitely try to keep to a well-planned session such as this one. I tend to feel safer when I know we have a clear idea of what we intend to do, though I recognize that as I grow more confident in my role as groupworker, I will feel more comfortable with less structure. Mullender and Ward (1989, p.8) rightly point out that the skill is to know what *not* to plan in advance because it is better left to be discussed with the group members. However, I would always prefer to plan a session well, and have the luxury of missing activities out, rather than struggle for 'time-fillers' during a session. One problem with this session was that it was jam-packed; in future, I would spend more time on group members' choices – the activities in the second half. Learning from the experience of this session, we decided that if we spent a lot of time one week on memory games, we would spend more time the next week on chosen activities, for example, cake decorating.

4.2 Action techniques

Description

Using the headings from 'Kaleidoscope' in Doel and Sawdon (1999, p.131) as a prompt, list all the techniques you have used during the life of the group. Pick out two specific examples and describe what you did in some detail.

Spoken word	Written word	Graphic
discussion	prompt cards	posters
reminiscence	questionnaires	photographs
oral history	logs	whiteboard

Hardware	Props	Movement
photography	smells	'chairobics'
tape recorder	crafts	throwing beanbag/ball
		darts
		tea/coffee breaks

Shape

full group

small groups

trios/pairs/individuals

PROMPT CARDS

We have used this action technique on several occasions. We used these cards in the 'Proverbs' game. Each group member was given a card which aided their participation in the game and gave them a reference point to join in the ensuing discussion. We also used prompt cards during a reminiscence activity, where the group was divided into small groups of two or three. Each group member had a piece of coloured card, on which were written three prompting questions about the Second World War, such as 'What do you remember about rationing?' Group members were encouraged to read the prompts on their cards and reminisce with their partners, using the prompts as a focus for discussion.

SMELLS

This is the only 'experimental' prop we have used in the life of the group so far. We found the idea for the 'Smells' game in a memory games book. We brainstormed ideas about which smells would be likely to evoke memories in older people, and decided on banana, lavender, cloves, TCP, lemon, hand cream, coffee and curry powder. I placed an example of each smell in a closed cup (with perforated lid) and labelled them 1–8. The group was divided into two (about five group members in each) and each group was given four smells. The groups were asked to nominate a scribe who would write down their group's consensus of what each smell was. We followed this with a discussion of what memories the smells evoked for individuals (pleasant? horrid?) and whether certain smells reminded them of being younger while others were associated with adulthood.

Analysis

Comment on the relative breadth or narrowness of the techniques you used – why was this?

Having written down all the action techniques we have used, it seems quite varied. As our group is activity-based, it has been necessary for us to offer a choice derived from what group members have said they would like to do, but which also stimulate and challenge group members, without being threatening. Heap (1985) writes that, in groups, action is often easier to initiate and take part in than discussion, and our group members have demonstrated this by responding better to games and situations where there is a physical activity involved (for example, throwing the beanbag). However, Heap (1985) cautions that an activity should always meet the need.

Reflection

Evaluate the examples of action techniques you have described – why did you use these particular techniques? How well did they achieve their purpose? What would you keep and change next time you use them?

Taking the examples of action techniques described above, I think the use of prompt cards does meet the need of the group members when engaging in discussions about long-term memory. We have been able to compare the differences in reminiscence sessions, for example, when we have been in a large group and asked the general question, 'What do you remember about the war?' Usually, one or two group members have dominated the discussion and the others have not been able to share their memories. However, using smaller groups and prompt cards making specific references to the war (e.g. rationing) has enabled less confident members to take part in an activity and feel valued.

Heap (1985, p.155) says activity should challenge group members in the area where their common problems affect their ability to function, and that 'joint achievement increases both cohesion and feelings of worth and mastery by the group as a whole'. The use of prompt cards has been successful in ensuring all group members are able to contribute to a memory game, increasing, we hope, self-esteem and a general feeling of group identity. I would keep every aspect of the prompt cards as an action technique, adapting the technique to fit the particular purpose.

The 'Smells' game was enjoyable, again focusing on stimulating memory, but in a lateral way which would not be perceived as testing. Crimmens (1998, p.23) notes that when the emphasis is on fun and social contact, people feel encouraged to relax more and 'begin to extend themselves without even thinking about it'. Using smells meant people had to interact more than usual, both with the object and with each other. The 'Smells' game did break down some barriers and certainly initiated discussion. However, there were also disadvantages in what we asked the group to do. First, we divided the group into two; unfortunately, one group consisted of two relatively new members and two fairly quiet members, while the other group consisted of the more dominant, talkative regulars. Thus, one group struggled to find a cohesive voice, and the members shrank away from choosing a scribe. This may have been disempowering for them, despite support from two groupworkers. Another problem was that some older people have a weakened sense of smell, which certainly limited their enjoyment of, and involvement in, the activity. However, they could still take part in the discussion about memories of smells.

The 'Smells' game was an experiment which we would not use again. There was some unease in taking part and the game was not especially inclusive. As an inexperienced groupworker, perhaps I did not want to take too many risks in case the group members were scared off. On reflection, perhaps I am still too unchallenging and want to please everyone. We could consider modifying the game by using touch to evoke memories as well. Group members could close their eyes and guess what certain objects are through touch, thus stimulating memory by using one of their other senses.

4.3 The work phase: issues of power and oppression

My experience of the work phase of this group has increased my awareness of the potential pitfalls in using action techniques in a group for people with memory problems, especially older people. We needed to find appropriate, non-oppressive ways of working with people with hearing problems, such as Peter, and not discriminating against him by everyone talking at once, or using large groups too much. 'For someone whose hearing is failing and who cannot keep up with a group discussion, a group activity may hold some anxiety' (Crimmens 1998, p.15).

Also, our use of prompt cards and the whiteboard could have been disempowering for those group members with a visual impairment, or whose literacy had deteriorated. In fact, we needed to recognize that some group members may not be able to read or write. We did attempt to re-evaluate our way of working by using large writing, and by checking out initially whether people were able to read in the first session by asking people to read names off the whiteboard. This is hard, as the exercise in itself could have been problematic for those experiencing difficulties in these areas. However, we felt it was necessary in order to plan our use of action techniques in the life of the group.

We tried lots of different action techniques as we wanted members to have the opportunity to achieve in whatever activity they chose. It was important for me to recognize that 'product-based' activities can disempower those who are unable to achieve the desired outcome (for example, painting straight lines due to impaired perception) and it was important to emphasize the fun and enjoyment of an activity. It was also important not to assume that older people with memory problems will necessarily enjoy reminiscence activities, so to offer choice. I was aware, too, of the male/female ratio in the group, and where power lies as a result of this. Fred, a dominant white male, holds gender power, and as a charismatic individual, holds personal power. However, as the rest of the group was mostly female, we held collective power which could have been threatening to Fred, particularly in our activities which tended to reflect women's roles.

Section 5

Group Processes

5.1 Individuals in the group

Description

Using the pen-pictures of the individual group members (Section1.3), describe the different kinds of role taken by individuals in the group; for example, a person who regularly provided 'internal leadership', a person who tended to be scapegoated in the group, etc.

Grace is one of the more dominant female members in the group. She is quite a 'mother figure' and tends to take other group members under her wing, particularly those whom she perceives as being less able than herself. Grace always ensures she sits near Jenny, and offers support, for example, mopping up Jenny's drink when she spills it through lack of coordination. Grace tends to dominate in reminiscence activities, as she has few other opportunities away from the group to express herself and talk about her past experiences.

Hannah is a regular member who plays second fiddle to Grace, but is clearly comfortable in this supporting role. Hannah sometimes has word-finding difficulties, and so prefers to let Grace speak for her. She will contribute to activities and discussions if she feels strongly about a subject. For example, in the 'Occasions' game, Hannah spent time talking about her wedding and the concept of marriage. Hannah obviously felt comfortable talking about this, but when she feels less certain, she lets others do the talking.

Peter is a quiet group member who nevertheless exudes an air of calm. Other group members pick up on this and Peter's presence builds a sense of safety and continuity in the group, as he always attends sessions and is willing to take part in activities.

Amanda does not interact much with other group members, but does hold power in the group through a sense of difference – she is always impeccably dressed and speaks with a West Country accent. Amanda tends to become more involved in activities she feels more able to do. She acted as a leader and spokesperson during the 'Proverbs' game (described earlier in Action Techniques).

Gillian only attended the group twice and did not take on any significant role. She was friendly and interactive with group members and groupworkers, but her absence has not affected the group as a whole.

Jane is another dominant female group member. Jane does not suffer from short-term memory problems to the extent of the other group members, and thus monopolizes the activities at times, as she is more articulate than the other group members and, like Grace, does not have the opportunity to express herself outside the group. Jane likes to be liked, often bringing in presents and raffle prizes, perhaps implying an underlying insecurity which could also explain her dominance.

Fred was the dominant male group member who attended regularly for several months. Fred provided the group with vibrancy and a sense of challenge, taking on the joking role; for example, in the 'name game', he told everyone his nickname, making it easy for people to remember him. Fred's presence is missed by the groupworkers, as he lent tension and sometimes conflict to the group, but group members, perhaps due to short-term memory problems, have not commented on his absence.

Jenny is a regular attender and, though quiet, gives the group a sense of identity. She has gradually opened up as each session has passed, and in conversations, has used 'we' and talks about 'our group'. Jenny is not a leader, but in her quiet way can demonstrate the group's cohesiveness through her own enjoyment of just being there. Jenny also takes on the role, perhaps unwillingly, of needing help from other members such as Grace.

Lily attends the group regularly. She is aware that she is less able than some other group members, and copes with this by playing the fool. Lily often compensates for making inappropriate comments by turning them into a joke, allowing herself and others to laugh. Her joking behaviour, then, is more defensive than Fred's. Lily and Jenny have a bond, perhaps because they both feel marginalized in the group.

Rita joined the group a few months after its inception, and has become a regular attender. Rita is self-assured and readily expresses any problems she experiences with her memory. In activities such as short-term memory games, Rita's willingness to share her problems is positive for other group members, while their acknowledgements and corroborations give Rita support in turn.

Analysis

Take two examples of behaviours in the group. What meaning do you think the behaviours had for the group, and was this helpful or hindering? Did you 'name' any of these situations (i.e. bring them into the open)?

DOMINATING BEHAVIOUR

In one particular session, Jane was monopolizing the discussion. Jane's superior short-term memory became starkly apparent during an activity which involved memorizing the objects on a tray before they were covered up, and then recalling as many as possible. Wanda and I were co-facilitating with a smaller group than usual, which is perhaps why Jane's dominant role was more obvious. We began by asking each group member in turn to recall one object from the tray, but inevitably, other group members chipped in, with Jane taking the lead.

Doel and Sawdon (1999, p.182) point out that 'it can be a fine line between a person who has been useful in starting the group off when other members are feeling reticent and withholding, and the next stage when group members are ready to participate but find they have lost the ground and are not allowed the opportunity to regain it'. Jane began the recall exercise, prompting others' memories, but took over the activity, exercising her own short-term memory, but not allowing other members the opportunity to take part. I think Jane feels it is important to be seen in a leadership or controlling role, perhaps because she does not feel in control of her home life, where she is overshadowed by her sons. She is also the most physically disabled member of the group, using a wheelchair; her exercise of mental pre-eminence might be a way of compensating for this.

I felt that Jane's behaviour was not helpful for the other group members, as they were not being given the opportunity to exercise their own short-term memories. However, I needed to be aware that the others could be colluding with Jane by letting her do the work, saving them the trouble! Benson (1987) suggests the value of openly acknowledging a group member's dominance, and therefore allowing it to becomes the group's concern. Wanda and I initially tried to manage this by asking everyone to take turns. When this failed, I suggested to Jane that I was aware of and impressed by her knowledge and recall, but wanted to give the others the same opportunity. I hoped Jane would feel her own contribution was valued, but would realize this was a group activity. Jane did tell June a few days later that she had been upset by my intervention, but it seemed the right approach at the time, as I did not feel Jane's role was helpful for the group as a whole.

SCAPEGOATING BEHAVIOUR

Douglas (1978, p.73) describes the scapegoat as 'a person who is obviously different from the others but who is also of value to the group and whose level of satisfaction is being met by his membership'. Doel and Sawdon (1999, pp.181–182) caution against personifying the behaviour (the scapegoat) and consider analysing the behaviour (scapegoating), which implicates the whole group and not just the one person. There has been some scapegoating in regard to Lily, who serves to create a more informal atmosphere for the group, as well as being of value to group members by making them feel secure because Lily offers herself as the butt of the joke which they might otherwise be. In the group, no one actually directs jokes at Lily – it is she who tends to make comments which do not automatically follow the discussion, and then make a joke of it.

It is difficult to gauge how comfortable Lily really feels with this situation. As a groupworker, I have found it difficult to 'name' any of the occurrences, for fear of drawing unwanted attention to Lily, and highlighting her perceived problems. Lily always manages to diffuse the potentially awkward silences caused by her seemingly inconsequential comments by making a joke, or laughing at herself, so we have felt it appropriate to let the moment pass.

Reflection

How did the individuals' behaviour in these examples make you feel? If you could script your response how would it differ from the reality of what happened?

I felt uncomfortable with Jane's dominance, as I felt it might be disempowering for the other group members, although I do recognize that the other members may not have felt this way. With hindsight, Wanda and I should have brought Jane's dominance into the discussion, as Benson (1987) suggests, in order to make the group own it, and decide what to do with it, rather than me feel personally responsible to do something about it. This would have been in line with Mullender and Ward's (1991, p.2) model of self-directed groupwork, where group members 'have the ability to frame their own problems, set their own goals and take their own action for change'.

In terms of the experience of scapegoating, I know Lily benefits from the group, as she has said so. Her pigeon-holing as the 'class clown' makes me feel concerned and challenges my groupwork skills. Should we weigh up the obvious benefits to the group of Lily's behaviour, with the possible damage to Lily's self-esteem? As such, we ensure we pick up after Lily has spoken, involving her and reorientating her as much as possible to the current discussion. Another approach we could take is that described by Whitaker (2000), who notes that a group member might talk about inconsequential topics as a first step to seeing how individual opinions will be tolerated within the group. On reflection, perhaps Lily's comments are a way of maintaining her own safety in the group.

5.2 Groupwork techniques

Description

Choose two of the 14 categories of groupwork technique adapted from Bertcher (1994). Describe these two techniques in detail by giving a specific example of each of them; quoted dialogue is the most effective way to do this, but don't worry if your memory isn't too accurate!

TECHNIQUE 1 : ATTENDING

Diane: OK, as you know, one of the purposes of coming to this group is to stimulate our memories, as we all forget things and get in a muddle from time to time…

Grace: Yes, I'm always forgetting what I've done five minutes ago…sometimes I can't even remember what day it is!

Hannah: I'm the same and it gets on my nerves – I'll be watching a programme on telly and suddenly it seems like I've missed what's been happening, so I don't bother watching any more.

Grace: I don't watch much telly now.

Diane: That must be very frustrating for you, Hannah.

Hannah: It gets me down.

Wanda: Do you do other things instead, then ?

Hannah: Yes, I do crayoning – Diane knows about that, don't you?

Diane: Yes, you said you find it therapeutic. It's a good form of stimulation and you enjoy it, which is the important thing.

Hannah: Sometimes people might think I'm childish, so I hide the drawing books!

Diane: But you find it helpful – I'm sure lots of us do things to help us when we're feeling down.

Grace: Well, I write things down to try and remember.

TECHNIQUE 2: GATE-KEEPING

Bella: On each of these cards is an 'occasion', for example, birthday, wedding, Christmas. We're going to hand out one each and then take it in turns to talk about what we have on our cards.

(June hands out cards.)

Jane: Oh, 'wedding' – well, I had two of those.

Diane: Did you really? Well, if everyone's got a card, you can start us off by telling us about that – it sounds intriguing!

(*Jane talks about her two weddings and the others chip in with their memories of their wedding days.*)

Diane: OK, shall we move on to another 'occasion' – what about you, Peter? What's on your card?

Peter: It says 'Christmas'.

Grace: Oh, I don't like Christmas much, it's lonely when you're on your own.

(*Several nods and murmurs of agreement*)

Jane: Well, it's for the children really, isn't it?

June: Does anyone remember Christmas as a child, then?

Jane: Ooh, yes…

Grace: But we didn't have much money of course…

Rita: You got oranges and things if there were lots of you…

Diane: It seems like Christmas stirs up good and bad feelings for most people – what do you think, Peter?

Peter: Well, I like Christmas, and I liked it as a kid, with the big dinner…

(*Everyone laughs.*)

Diane: Is there anything else you like about it?

Peter: No, not that I remember now.

Analysis

Taking these two pieces of quoted dialogue in turn, what do you think was most effective and least effective about them? Re-write the dialogue as you would prefer it to have been.

I have used the first description as an example of the 'Attending' technique. Bertcher (1994) says attending is a way of paying close attention to what a group member is saying, often to the exclusion of other group members, by using eye contact and open body language. In this example, I had begun by reiterating one of the main purposes of the group, and intended to go on to describe a memory game. However, Grace began a potential discussion by sharing her own experience of short-term memory problems. She often does this and it is useful for other group members, as they feel they are not alone in their problems. In this instance, Hannah picked up on Grace's theme and shared an example of her short-term memory problems, directing what she was saying to me. She also expressed her feelings about this; 'it gets on my nerves', 'it gets me down'. Although Grace chipped in again, I wanted Hannah to elaborate on her feelings as I felt she needed some reassurance, so I focused my attention on what she was saying and encouraged her to say more by using empathy in my response.

Hannah often supports other members' comments but does not often speak out unsolicited on her own, and I wanted to encourage this in order to help her, if I could. I think my empathizing comment was effective in that it enabled Hannah to express how she felt, but I also feel Wanda's 'attending' worked in that she diverted Hannah away from feeling down and enabled her to describe a helping technique which could be useful for the whole group. I think this 'attending' was a positive way of encouraging Hannah to share more within the group, but with hindsight, I could have encouraged her to talk more about why her short-term memory problems made her feel down, opening the discussion up to the group, asking them to support Hannah.

'Attending' is a useful tool in groupwork, but it does not conform to the self-help model of groupwork where the members support each other. Instead of directing her comments to the group, Hannah directed them at me. Perhaps she felt safer doing this, since I am her social worker, as well as one of the groupworkers, and she has talked about her problems with me before. This need for safety should be respected. However, I could have encouraged her to talk to Grace, or indeed to the whole group, if they had been willing to offer support. All too often, group members look to the four of us for support, rather than to each other, increasing the power divide and the sense that we have the answers, rather than the answers being with the group.

In rewriting the dialogue, I would have liked Hannah to share her feelings and to have directed her comments to the group:

Hannah: It gets me down – I bet I'm not the only one who feels like this?

Rita: It's the same for me – I'd rather go out and do something else, like going to Bingo.

The second description is an example of the 'Gate-keeping' technique which, in common with my co-workers, I found myself using quite often. The group members all experience memory problems, but some find it more difficult than others to interact in a group setting and often certain group members can monopolize the discussion, which means others do not get the opportunity to participate. There are a few group members, namely Jane and Grace, who do not have much opportunity to express themselves outside of the group, and so they relish the opportunity to talk at length within the group setting. These two group members also find reminiscence activities particularly stimulating, as they can recall many experiences.

When Bella stipulated that each person would have a particular 'occasion' to talk about, and that we would take it in turns, she set the scene for 'group members from social groups who are traditionally seen as lower participators to play their part' (Doel and Sawdon 1999, p.171); for example, those experiencing hearing problems or more long-term memory problems, or who, through past experiences, feel less empowered to contribute. This was effective, and it was appropriate that Jane should begin, since dominant members do have a positive role in getting people started in an activity. I wanted to involve Peter, as he didn't participate in the 'wedding' discussion, perhaps because he has never been married. However, Peter's participation was again overshadowed by the others, and it was quite difficult to draw him into the discussion, although he did eventually share his experiences. The group laughter may have deterred him from further contributions.

With hindsight, this was an example of 'gate-keeping' which did not take into account how Peter might feel about talking within the large group, in which he was the only male. Perhaps we could have used smaller groups to do the activity, where Peter may have felt more able to contribute. Also, Peter has a hearing impairment, and it can be confusing for him when a number of people speak at once. Instead of using the spoken word, we could have used other techniques to promote broader participation, for example, the whiteboard.

I could have tried to extended Peter's involvement in this way:

Diane: It seems like Christmas stirs up good and bad feelings for most people – what do you think, Peter?

Peter: Well, I like Christmas, and I liked it as a kid, with the big dinner…

(*Everyone laughs*)

Diane: What do you like about Christmas these days, Peter?

Peter: I like it now when all the decorations are up and in the shops – I think it's really cheerful.

Reflection

Taking your groupwork style overall, which of the 14 techniques do you use best and which do you think you need to improve?

I use several interactional techniques regularly in the group, and 'gate-keeping' is one of these. It helps to have co-workers in these situations, as there are more of us to facilitate sub-group discussion, or ensure that everyone has the opportunity to participate. When one person is dominating or talking to one groupworker, another groupworker can observe this process and open it up to the wider group. I also regularly 'negotiate and reinforce' the group agreement with the group members, particularly at the start of each session. Despite the problems described in the previous example, I feel I use these techniques appropriately, and hone them with experience.

'Attending' is often a one-to-one approach, used in counselling, and I feel the skill is to focus attention on the individual, while also being aware of group dynamics. I have used this technique successfully on some occasions, but again, it helps to have a co-worker who is in tune with the rest of the group and can integrate the one-to-one interaction into a discussion involving the whole group.

Reflecting on my rewritten section on 'Attending' in the Analysis section, I realise that I focused on how I would have liked Hannah to have behaved, rather than on what I did as a groupworker. A significant aspect of my role is to support and encourage group members to speak out, and to develop confidence, and I need to recognize that my actions and interactions as a groupworker guide group members' behaviour and thoughts. Therefore, rather than responding to Hannah's comment about her crayoning by giving *my* interpretation about what it means to her, I could have encouraged her to share this coping strategy with the whole group, in this way:

Hannah: Yes, I do crayoning – Diane knows about that, don't you?

Diane: Yes, and you said you find it helpful. It would be really useful if you could share with the others what it is about crayoning that you enjoy, and how it helps you.

I could have used minimal encouragers (head nods, etc.) to support Hannah, and Wanda and I could then have encouraged other group members to share their coping strategies.

I was about to change the text in the previous section (Analysis), but decided to leave it in to give me the opportunity to demonstrate here how my understanding has developed during my work on this portfolio.

Summarizing is not one of my strong points, although I have often tried to draw together the diverse threads in an activity to inform group goals, for example, at the end of a session, when the group is reflecting on their feelings about it. I have struggled at times, and would like to consider using different action techniques to aid summary, perhaps using graphics or diagrams to show what the group has achieved, rather than just talking about it.

I do use the 'Rewarding' technique, and have reflected on when and whether this is appropriate. The emphasis of the group is stimulation through enjoyable activities; to 'balance the prevailing attitudes of negativity towards older people with an emphasis on what people can do rather than what they cannot' (Crimmens 1998, p.22). However, in a group of mixed abilities, some people are inevitably able to do and achieve more than others. I revert to a kind of reverse-favouritism, focusing on those who have more problems with their memories, and encouraging them in activities through acknowledgement of their achievements, however small. A sense of achievement is relative to an individual's personal goals, and when a group member's self-esteem has been increased, this contributes to a group sense of satisfaction.

5.3 Group themes

Description

Describe what you understand by Doel and Sawdon's (1999, pp.195–204) notion of Group Themes, giving one or two specific examples from your group.

Doel and Sawdon's (1999) notion of group themes is linked to Shulman's (1984) concept of the 'two clients', which relates to the consideration of the needs of individuals in the group, alongside the needs of the group as a whole. It is about exploring and working with individual feelings while remaining aware of the collective feelings of the group and how they are affected by this. The two clients are the 'I', each person as an individual, and the 'we', the group as a collectivity (Doel and Sawdon 1999, p.198).

An example of working with the 'two clients' was when Fred arrived at the group in a really bad mood. He refused to speak to anyone when he entered the room and the look on June's face showed that she was concerned about him (she had picked him up in her car). Fred was talking under his breath about his sister and when I said hello to him, he asked me where his sister was. I said that I did not know, that she was not here, but that we were pleased to see Fred here. Fred sat down with the others, but closed his eyes, shutting us out. We had planned to start the session with an ice-breaker game where group members take it in turn to throw the beanbag at laminated questions on the floor. Each card had a series of related questions on it, which would prompt group discussion. The three of us (June, Wanda and I – Bella was absent) intended to scatter ourselves amongst the group and assist the group members in the game. However, Fred's obvious mood could not be ignored, as other group members were looking at him in concern.

Wanda and I moved over to sit next to Fred, asking him if he felt OK, would he like a drink, etc., which prompted two other group members to come over and express their concern. By making eye contact, Wanda and I were aware that we may have been crowding Fred and also heightening group anxiety that something was not right. June, who was observing, commented to me that Fred was not feeling very well. This allowed me to ask Fred if this was so, to which he nodded. Wanda asked if he felt comfortable on that chair – again the nod – so we felt able to begin the session. By using eye contact and a slight rearrangement of the room, we ensured Wanda sat on one side of Fred and Grace on the other. Grace had eased the situation by stating that Fred must have a headache, which explained to the other group members why he was sitting with his eyes shut.

Instead of beginning the session immediately, June asked if everyone else was feeling all right, and commented that it was a very warm day. I made a comment about headaches in thundery weather, and several other group members agreed that hot weather made them feel uncomfortable. This shifted our attentions from Fred as an individual with a 'problem' to the abstract idea of weather, which everyone could discuss. We then felt able to begin the game, and Fred, no longer the focus of the group, began to relax and join in gradually.

Analysis

Was the group able to move from a collection of 'I's to a feeling of 'we'? How did you help the individuals in the group to become 'a group'?

The four of us have discussed, when recording the groupwork, what roles different members take on, and what kind of power various group members hold. I have always felt that Fred holds a lot of power in the group and that he is quite a dominant member, mainly because he is one of the two men in the group, and Peter, the other man, is usually quiet. Fred, on the other hand, is physically a big man, who is often jovial and vocal in the group. I have noticed that some of the other group members, especially Grace and Hannah, go out of their way to involve and chat to Fred, and that we groupworkers, especially Wanda and I, are particularly concerned that Fred takes part in and enjoys the group.

I think my feelings described above definitely influenced the way I handled this example of the 'two clients', and I know I would have acted differently if it had been Peter or a female member who had come to the session as Fred did. Part of this is owing to the fact that Fred has often mis-interpreted conversations and situations, caused by his memory problems and possibly a hearing impairment. When this has occurred, Fred has needed reassurance and the group activity has continued. However, the four of us were aware that we do not know Fred well (he was referred by one of the community teams) and we have never quite been able to predict his reactions. I realize that I have always wanted to keep Fred interested in activities for fear that he becomes bored or irritable. I know that this is partly caused by my own fear of facing conflict in the group situation, as I am a new groupworker and I am working to overcome this fear. Also, Fred is in a minority in the group and I am constantly aware of the male/female ratio and the need to tailor our activities to meet the needs of both genders. I am aware that I have fallen into the trap of stereotyping Fred as a big man and therefore a potential for aggression when bored or misinterpreting events. However, the acknowledgement of this failing on my part makes it easier for me to evaluate why I acted as I did in the described example.

When Fred came in, it was clear that all was not well with him. I wanted to know how he was, and was able to pick up from June's nonverbal communication that Fred was upset about something. When he asked me where his sister was, it seemed that he was disorientated and looking for reassurance. I wanted Fred to feel welcome and comfortable in the group, but also wanted him to be able to talk about what was upsetting him. I was trying to elicit information from him about his feelings, and also show empathy for his distress. With hindsight, it may have been easier for Fred if we had allowed him to join in the group when he was ready, without putting pressure on him to 'share'. We did not feel we could ignore the issue, as the other group members had picked up the atmosphere, which is why Wanda and I turned our attentions on him. However, this excluded other group members and probably hindered Fred's ability to express his feelings. It was very useful that June was observing the situation as a whole. She tuned in to the general group feeling and made an innocuous comment about Fred 'not feeling well'. This immediately made Fred's behaviour more acceptable to the group members, and certain people such as Grace expressed more warmth towards Fred because of this.

I feel June's actions smoothed over a potential 'sticky moment', and also moved the focus away from the individual and back to the group as a whole. The group were given the opportunity to identify with Fred through their own experiences, and thus the issue of headaches and ill health became a group theme, not just Fred's problem. I hope that the ensuing discussion also sent out the message that it was OK to bring concerns, distress or problems to the group, and that people would still be accepted and welcomed if they were feeling out of sorts or argumentative. I think this example was instrumental in the building of a group identity, through the explicit sharing of common problems, and the implicit acceptance of group members who upset the status quo, however temporarily. 'The feelings level, though not necessarily articulated in words, should not be underestimated as a powerful factor in helping individuals to become a group' (Doel and Sawdon 1999, p.204).

Reflection

Are there any other themes which you have identified subsequently? Was the notion of 'group themes' useful in helping you to facilitate the group's move from 'I' to 'we'?

The above example also heightened a central theme and aim of the group – to improve self-esteem and enhance abilities in a social setting. Heap (1985, p.123) feels that 'Western industrial societies infantilize, de-individualize and alienate their aged, ascribing them roles of such dependence and passivity as to shatter their self-esteem and their social health'. He feels that conflict, tension and challenge are important if dealt with sensitively, as conflict can be an important source of self-assertion and esteem for older people.

It would have been useful to check out with the group if they felt their shared experiences of short-term memory problems was instrumental in moving from 'I' to 'we'. Although this is the most obvious emergent theme in the group, I feel the group members moved towards a sense of commonality and belonging through their support of each other, which has been both explicit and implicit. An example of explicit support is when Grace affirms other group members' experiences by stating she has the same problems, thus making the other group members feel less isolated; and implicit support is illustrated by the 'mothering' which Grace and Hannah show towards Fred when he is clearly in some distress.

The notion of a group theme is useful, but I am uncertain how successful I was in helping the group to address possible underlying themes, such as fear of what the future held.

5.4 Group processes: issues of power and oppression

The definitions of individuals as 'dominant' or 'well dressed' are themselves laden with power – who makes the definitions? We could be using our power as professionals to label people who already suffer from the 'people with memory problems' tag. People enact certain roles in order to manage other people's expectations of them. Individuals labelled with memory problems or dementia will develop certain expectations, 'that they will be treated as less than they have learned to expect of and for themselves, and that the frustration of these ingrained expectations is due to the possession of an attribute that functions as a social stigma' (Goffman 1967, p.267). I needed to be conscious of this in my groupwork, not to exacerbate the powerlessness of people who already experience discrimination in society. 'Elderly people have very low expectations of the quality of their lives after repeated experiences of loss and bereavement' (Mullender 1990, p.292). It is difficult to prevent dominance while at the same time showing understanding of why some group members emerge as dominant.

It has been important to acknowledge that groups do not exist in isolation and that our group is a social microcosm, where the reproduction of external social attitudes takes place and can continue, if left unacknowledged and unchallenged. For example, when I worked to involve Peter in the discussion, was I conforming to a female role of looking after the needs of men, or was I trying to include a group member who has hearing problems and memory impairment?

We needed to be constantly aware of the kinds of power which we, as groupworkers, were invested with, such as the formal authority of our role as groupworkers, the professional authority which is associated with expertise and knowledge, and the impact of our difference (unlike group members, we are not elderly and do not experience memory loss). Within the group leadership there are power imbalances, and it was necessary to understand what impact this might have on group processes.

We have not addressed issues of race directly. We are an all-white group, which does mean that race is not 'present', but the group has not been directly confronted with issues of race and racism. Issues of ageism and disability have been much more pressing for the group members. In terms of gender, as an all-women leadership, this could be seen as positive, with women in an empowering role.

Section 6

Endings

6.1 Session endings

Description

Take one of the sessions of your group to describe how you ended it.

In this particular session, Wanda and I co-worked, since June was on holiday and Bella was on duty in the office. The group members had not split up into smaller groups for crafts or games as there were only two facilitators, and so we had focused on a short-term memory game, a long-term memory game, tea/coffee break, a game of bingo, a raffle and a game of darts. With 5–10 minutes left, we asked the group as a whole if they had enjoyed the session. Everyone nodded or said yes, as is usual with the group members. I have never heard them disagree. I then said that Wanda and I thought it would be useful to reflect on what we have done in this particular session, and to say one thing that particularly stands out from the session.

We asked the group members if anyone could remember how we had begun the session. No-one responded, so Wanda offered a prompt to Peter to help him remember. While he thought, some of the other group members commented on how difficult it was to remember right back to the start of the session. Peter eventually asked if we had started with the 'name game', so I said that although that was not in this session, we had done it last week, so it was positive that he could remember part of last week's session. Jane chipped in that we had started with the 'Tray' game, remembering objects on a tray. Everyone immediately agreed, and Rita commented that she had found the game difficult. When I asked her if she

114

could say some more, she commented that she found it hard to remember most of the activities we had done. Wanda opened this up to the group; was this the same for other group members? Grace and Jenny agreed.

I then asked Jenny if she could remember any other aspects of the session and she said the game of darts. Lily made a joke about her contribution to the game and everyone laughed, easing the tension which had been caused by the others worrying about not being able to remember. I stressed that the purpose of reflecting was not to test the group members, but to focus ourselves on the session and whether we have achieved our aims of stimulating memories. The group members agreed that it was important to do this, as it helped to remind them of the reason they came to the group in the first place.

Analysis

Evaluate the session ending which you have described. Was the ending planned the way it happened? If so, why did you plan it this way – what were your aims for this session ending? What aspects were most, and what least, successful about this ending? It what ways was it typical or untypical of other session endings?

In the early stage of the group, several sessions did not have formal endings. In these sessions, more typically the ones where group members spent the latter half of the session involved in diverse activities, we would lose track of time and it would suddenly be four o'clock. We would then make motions to leave; some group members, such as Amanda, are aware of the time and know their husbands or carers will be expecting them home. It always felt as though we were drifting away from a session, without really drawing it to a close or summarizing the feelings of what we have achieved, as individuals and as a group.

Because of this, we decided to be more aware of the passing of time, and to regroup at the end of a session in order to sum up. Benson (1987) states that endings are vital in teaching group members how to develop coping strategies. Endings can minimize emotional fallout from the session. In my example, it was important to restate to group members that one of the main aims of the session was to help find ways of coping with memory problems through the sharing of experiences, and not through the testing of skills. I think that the main aim of summing up was to focus the group members on what had been achieved in the session, but this proved difficult in our group, as asking group members to discuss the session immediately divided the group into those who could remember and those who could not. This could have been very disempowering and was not the desired outcome for our ending, so we used interactional techniques to involve the whole group in a reflection on the session. Wanda used the techniques of 'seeking information' and 'gatekeeping' to include Peter in the session, which I feel was very successful, as he is quite a reticent group member. I saw his contribution as very positive because even though he did not remember that particular session, he could recall an activity from the previous session. I used the 'rewarding' technique to demonstrate to the group that members were beginning to reach group goals (stimulation of memory, in any form).

The fact that much of this ending was led by group members, albeit implicitly, was the most successful aspect. Wanda and I did not have to facilitate much, and the group members themselves said that they recognized the importance of 'checking-out' in reminding them of why they were there. The session ending described earlier highlights the problems involved in reflecting for people with memory problems, but also the ways in which they can help each other, through understanding and a sense of group identity. Grace had said, 'We're all in the same boat'.

Another way of aiding the ending process would be to use a version of our prompt cards; we could use visual prompts depicting each part of the session and show them to the group members to stimulate recall, or we could ask group members to make a visual or written note of each part of the session as it occurs, to use as a memory jogger in the later summing up and checking out.

Reflection

How did you find out what group members felt about a session? In what ways were group members' feelings similar or different from each others' and from yours?

Jane, Rita and Lily helped to focus the whole group on the different aspects of summing up, although in different ways. Jane was able to prompt the group about the session's activities, Rita was able to allow other group members the safety to acknowledge their memory problems, and Lily lightened the atmosphere by making everyone laugh, which is always a good note to end on. 'Humour is the group's salt and pepper' (Doel and

Sawdon 1999, p.186), and 'there is no better publicity for your group than people coming out looking and sounding as if they have had a really good time' (Crimmens 1998, p.22).

In this particular session ending, some group members volunteered information about how they felt about the session; for example, Rita said she found it hard and I asked her to elaborate. The fact that everyone says yes when we ask whether they have enjoyed the group is not necessarily a sign of the group's success. Older people often find it difficult to voice dissent or complain – 'the need for care makes it impossible to "bite the hand that feeds"' (Mullender 1990, p.291). The group strives to challenge this indictment of services for older people, by promoting opportunities for group members to 'opt out' of activities and state their preferences. On the other hand, it may be that all group members genuinely *do* enjoy the sessions and have no complaints.

6.2 Group endings

Description

If the group was time-limited, describe the last session of the group and how you and/or group members planned the ending. If the group is open-ended, describe how an individual group member has left the group. If neither of these has happened, describe how you and group members see the group functioning in, say, six months' time.

Our group is open-ended, but several members have left the group during its lifetime. I think the most significant absence in the group is Fred, but his absence is felt more by the four of us than by the group members. Fred did not leave the group formally, but chose not to come back, despite the efforts of the groupworkers. We never verbalized to the group that Fred had chosen not to attend the group, as he did not give us a reason, and no-one has asked us why he does not come any more. Perhaps the other group members have not been affected by his absence, or perhaps they do not feel comfortable voicing a recognition of his absence. Perhaps this is seen as failure or rejection from their point of view, in that he chose not to be in their company; from our point of view, in that he is dismissing the service; or from the point of view of the group, in that it is not meeting his needs. I prefer to see his absence as an exercise of choice, and perhaps an affirmation of the group's aim to promote independence and self-esteem. Fred may feel that he does not need to attend the group any more. I hope this is true.

Analysis

How successful was the group ending and how did you evaluate this? (NB Success of the group overall is discussed in the next section). If the group is open-ended, how are you monitoring its effects?

I see the group as continuing with the same objectives in six month's time, although the continuation of the group depends on several factors:

- Is the group achieving its goals and making a difference in the lives of the individuals who attend the group? Do the group members feel the group is meeting their needs? We hope to show this through the group evaluation process. Certainly, the questionnaires (appended to the original portfolio) indicate that they are keen for the group to continue.

- Are Bella and I are able to remain involved with the group to the extent that we have been? Other work pressures and management directives might withdraw us from the group leadership. This would be a significant 'ending' for the group, though we hope not an end for the group, since June, Wanda and Marie, the other support worker in the team, can continue to facilitate the group.

Working within a model of self-directed groupwork, we would like to see the group develop a strong sense of its own identity, and perhaps to work with outside agencies such as the Alzheimer's Disease Society or Age Concern, in order to raise awareness of the issues surrounding memory problems. Brown (1994, p.158) urges us to 'consider at all times the possibility of the group actively engaging in efforts to effect environmental change'. However, we would also need to respect the right of group members to refuse, and their wish to keep the group as it is.

Reflection

What do you feel is the main purpose of group endings? If the group has ended, what impact has this had on you? If the group is continuing, do you see a time for your own personal ending with this group?

Group endings are the opportunity for group members and groupworkers to bring together all that has been achieved over the life of the group, and celebrate the positive outcomes, both collectively and for individuals. Endings are also a time for everyone with a stake in the group to evaluate it, in terms of their thoughts and feelings about the group, whether people feel it has been successful, what people liked and what they would change. Our group was open-ended, but, as explained earlier, we tried to ensure that each session had an ending, which we hoped would become a conscious ritual.

Despite the group being open-ended, we have always known that some of the workers (primarily myself and Bella) would have to leave the group, due to other work commitments. This was discussed with group members at the outset, as we wanted everyone to feel prepared for this inevitable transition. We had to be careful to balance this need for preparation with the insecurity which group members might feel as a result of this. However, we have always encouraged the group members to feel safe in the group, with the desire that the support that they derive from each other would enhance a feeling of security, independent of the workers.

Saying 'goodbye' is important, and I would like my ending to be marked by a celebration. As Doel and Sawdon (1999, p.263) point out, 'some groups, especially long-running ones, may have rehearsed "celebration" at other times during the life of the group'. This is true of our group. We have always made a point of celebrating birthdays, with a cake and a bottle of sparkling wine as a present. There needs to be room for people to share sad feelings too. I shall be sad to leave the group as it has been a valuable and enjoyable experience for me, and an opportunity for development, both personally and professionally.

6.3 Endings: issues of power and oppression

The biggest issue around endings, in terms of anti-oppressive groupwork, is how are endings decided? Groupworkers have to be honest about the amount of time they can give to a group, and group members need to know this from the outset. Group members also need to know what their obligations are, in terms of a commitment to see a group out to the end, or to be able to come and go as they choose. *Memory Joggers* is an open-ended group, so members know they can leave the group whenever they choose; in some respects group members like Fred, who left without explanation, can hold quite a lot of power over the group even in their absence. However, I think this is more in our minds as groupworkers than in group members' thoughts.

I hope to make my own transition from the group as empowering as possible. In part, this has meant being clear early on that Bella and I will not be able to stay with the group indefinitely; it is important that group members don't harbour any fantasies that we are leaving because 'we don't like the group'.

Evaluating the Group

7.1 Recording the groupwork

Description

Briefly describe the pattern of your groupwork recording. Include an example of the recording you did as part of the groupwork, stating when the recording was done and which session of the group it refers to.

At the end of each session, after we have taken everyone home, washed the dishes and tidied the room, the group leadership sits down together and, using a 'Groupwork log' template, we reflect on our thoughts and feelings about the session. June and I have taken it in turns to do the actual writing.

The example recording (Figure 8) was done after Session 15 of the group on Monday 19 July at 4.50 pm in our office.

Analysis

Comment on the way you decided to record your groupwork and what other choices were available to you. What was the main purpose of the example piece of recording you have included? How did you and/or group members use it?

Name of the group: *Memory Joggers*

My name: *Diane Morrison*

Session number: *15*

Who was present and who sat where? – draw a diagram in the box.

Date and time of session: *19 July 2–4 pm*

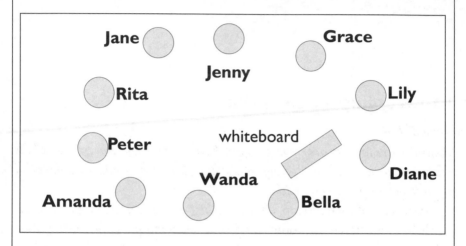

If somebody was absent, do you know why? Is there a need to follow up? *Fred would not come.*

Consider who contributed most? *(Jane)* – least? *(Peter)* Is there a pattern? Where does power lie in the group? *Jane was most powerful – this week her memory was very intact*

What were the main aims of this session?

1. *Memory Tray Game–aimed to help members talk more openly about memory problems and share coping strategies. Fun, too.*

2. *Four Seasons Game–to engage people as a group and encourage interaction.*

3. *Darts Game–physical activity to help coordination and provide stimulation. Different people have different talents.*

What themes are emerging for the group?

1. *Loss–primarily of memory and therefore of a sense of self and of 'being', but also loss of friends.*

2. *Group Identity–more apparent because smaller group this week? A few people using 'we'; and more direct exchanges between individual members–not using leaders as a 'switchboard'.*

3. *Sharing.*

What was the general atmosphere and feeling of this session of the group?

There was a really good sense of belonging - possibly because it was a smaller group this session? Jenny was quite forward and chatty this week, not so overpowered by Jane. Amanda is starting to be more open and seems to be coming to terms with her memory problems. Grace becoming 'possessive' over Peter?!

What was my main contribution to the session? What did my co-leader particularly contribute?

This session was facilitated mainly by me, with Wanda and Bella joining the last half. We shared responsibilty for running the two memory exercises. I felt OK about the balance, but didn't get the chance to check this out with the others (am I too dominant?). Bella made a couple of specific interventions which helped Amanda open up.

What I learned most from this session as a group leader was...

The importance of summing up. This focuses the group members on what they have done (most have already forgotten). It also struck me starkly how memory ability is the main definer of power in this group (hence Jane's strength in the group this session).

Future plans include...

A trip out? Group members have mentioned this – they don't have much opportunity to visit places. It helps people to feel 'connected' to the everyday world. Also, the four of us need to reflect on those aspects of sessions which help individuals to interact with each other, to build on the sense of belonging which is developing.

Figure 8 Groupwork log

We began recording our groupwork after the first session, and made firm promises to each other that, whatever happened, we would always make time after a session to debrief, by reflecting on the session. This entailed discussion of each group member, the group as a whole, and an evaluation of our own practice. We used the 'Groupwork log', devised by Doel and Sawdon (1999, p.236), as it combines written word with graphics, and description with pointers for analysing our groupwork. Although we faithfully make time for recording, we are not as reflective as I would like, and our groupwork recording tends to contain more description than evaluation.

We knew we needed to record our groupwork in order to retain some of the immediacy of the sessions, to have available when we came to evaluate the group formally. We were not told we had to keep written records of the group for agency purposes, but we recognized the need to account for our group, and evidence that we had evaluated it. This is perhaps why we chose to stick to the conventional format of recording in written prose; being new to groupwork, I was also a little nervous of attempting more creative approaches. In a self-directed model of groupwork, recording would be a group activity; its format decided upon and undertaken by the group members themselves. Throughout the life of the group, I have found it hard to reconcile our group to this model, but as Doel and Sawdon (1999, p.234) point out, 'the act of recording can be creative and an integral part of the group itself'. With hindsight, we could have used flipcharts throughout all our memory games (we used a whiteboard, as this is what was available), and kept the flipcharts as a record capturing the essence of the group.

In one sense, we have all shared the task of recording through our activities. For example, we devised a birthday board in one session, where we took a Polaroid picture of everyone, including ourselves, and discussed various aspects of our lives (for example, date of birth, star sign, important events). These were all written on separate pieces of A3 paper with the group member's name in the middle, and the photo next to it. These pieces of group history are pinned on the wall for each session and taken down afterwards to protect confidentiality. Moreover, the group room is adorned with half-painted glasses, completed plant pots and half-finished jigsaws – all a kind of record of 'groupwork in progress'.

Reflection

Which aspects of your recording would you keep and which would you change if you were to run this kind of group again?

I would keep the regular time set aside at the end of each session to record our thoughts, and to discuss how we feel about the session as groupworkers. However, our recording is often rushed, and, looking back, the recording of some sessions does not give a clear picture of what happened during the session, either at an explicit or implicit level. This applies to individuals and the whole group. Often, we focus too much on activities and not on what has been achieved *as a group*. Also, I must consider how to involve group members themselves in the recording of the group; although we have discussed our record-keeping with them, they have never seen any examples of it. In the same way that we now all come together at the end of each group session to 'check out', we could use this time to record, too, perhaps by collecting reflections of the session on a flipchart.

Comment on the example piece of recording. What is its main purpose? How did you and/or group members use it? How might you have done it differently?

The main purpose of the example piece of recording (Figure 8) is to outline the structure and group dynamics of one session. The diagram is particularly useful to me as I can immediately visualize the layout of the room, who was present and who they most related to. It also reminds me how and why we set out the room, and informs future planning; the layout of the room encouraged the group to interact more closely with each other, so we should use it more often.

This example of our recording also demonstrates certain patterns in terms of group processes. For example, I notice from different logs that there is a recurring pattern of Jenny and Peter possibly feeling overpowered by others, though Jenny is less so in this particular session. This remains a speculation, but I now wonder what impact this might have on Jenny and Peter's enjoyment of the group. Does it signify a power imbalance in our group?

I think that 'sharing' as a theme is too vague, and I needed to elaborate what this means. I could have concentrated on recognizing and acknowledging short-term memory problems, which is a predominant theme. In terms of 'aims', I initially described the pros and cons of each action technique used. On reflection, I understood that the aims were what underpinned the action techniques – in other words, why did we choose to use them specifically? This was helpful in being explicit with co-workers about future action techniques and our aims in using them.

I think the 'co-worker' section works effectively, though it is brief. Although I have not been explicit about the interactional technique which Bella used, it is a useful reminder to me, as is the note to check out my co-workers' view of my level of involvement.

In general, I think this piece of recording reflects the mood of the session accurately. It fulfils a number of different purposes and helps both our review and our planning for the group. The next step is actively to involve group members in this process of recording.

7.2 Evaluation

Description

Take each group member in turn and describe the impact of the group on them, giving specific examples of the evidence on which your description is based. Has the experience of the group led to any particular changes in behaviour, attitudes, life style, etc., outside the group?

    See Section 1.3: 'Pen pictures' for an initial overview of each individual member.

An important factor in evaluating the group is to consider who has an interest in it – the 'stakeholders'. The group members are the major stakeholders, and we wanted to find out what personal impact the group has had on their lives. We have done this through the use of a questionnaire and, with members' permission, by talking to other professionals involved with individual members and with their relatives and carers. In some cases, we have visited individual members at home.

Grace's community psychiatric nurse has noticed a change in the way Grace copes at home. She is less anxious about her memory problems and needs fewer visits from the CPN . Also, since coming to the group, she has been discharged from the outpatients clinic.

Hannah is my individual client and she has told me that the group is 'just what she needed' and how much she looks forward to Monday afternoons.

Peter's community carer contacted us to tell us that when she visits him each Monday evening, he talks about the group and sometimes about what he has done.

Amanda's husband has pointed out that, prior to attending the group, she was quite 'up and down', but has not displayed this behaviour since the group started.

Gillian unfortunately could not continue with the group as she became too frail.

Jane is Bella's client and has often told Bella how much she values being with the other group members. Jane's son has also said he appreciates what the group does for his mum.

Fred seemed to enjoy the group at first, but he chose to leave so we were unable to find out what impact the group had on his life.

Jenny's self-confidence has increased and she contributes to group conversations now, whereas before she tended to stay in the background. Her husband said Jenny never complains about getting ready for the group, compared with other day services, which she refuses to attend.

Lily's husband says he is able to use the time when Lily is at the group to do household chores so he is able to spend more quality time with Lily when she comes home.

Rita's son has told us that she always seems brighter when she comes home from the group.

Analysis

What methods did you use to evaluate the group? How effective were these?

Evaluation 'should be a recurrent theme during the group's life, as worker and group members review progress, and if necessary, redefine goals and methods' (Brown 1994, p.197). The immediate feedback of attendance and expressions of enjoyment from group members build a picture as to whether the group is meeting its aim of encouraging social interaction. The weekly log (Figure 8) has also been an important evaluative tool.

In our recent review, we used a questionnaire as part of a session, explaining to group members that we all needed to know how they felt about the group's progress, so we could continue to meet their needs within the group. We decided to give out the questionnaires in the session and talk the group members through it, giving assistance to those who needed it. Of course, there is no way of confirming whether it is the group which has helped these members achieve changes in their lives, but the questionnaires clearly indicate their enjoyment in attending. As the group is open-ended, we plan to evaluate the group in three months, assuming the group can continue, and will use a questionnaire.

As described earlier, we have obtained comments from 'significant others', such as Rita's son and Amanda's husband. At a later date, and with group members' permission, it could be useful to devise questionnaires for professionals and for carers, to find out their views about any longer-term effects of the group on its members. However, it is as well to recognize that feedback may not always be positive. For example, if the group has aided someone in increasing their self-esteem, they may be more assertive at home, which could be seen as a problem from the point of view of a relative or carer.

It has been particularly important for the four of us to evaluate the 'success' (a relative term) of the group in order to present the results to the rest of the Community Mental Health Team, so that we can argue for the need for the group to continue. 'Part of the group's credibility comes from its ability to articulate what has worked and what has not worked' (Doel and Sawdon 1999, p.237). In the Reflection section, I look at how my analysis of how these findings can be best presented has developed.

Reflection

In what ways has the group worked as a group, as opposed to a collection of individuals? What part do you feel you have played in helping the group achieve its purposes?

In order to evaluate the group, I considered three aspects: the group as a whole, each individual member, and my development as a groupworker. I think the best example of the group working together rather than as a collection of individuals is in our 'summing up' at the end of each session, when group members are invited to reflect on their achievements and feelings in a particular session and in the group as a whole. This helps us all to make links between individual feelings and achievements and the group as a group. However, memory problems make it a challenge to include all group members in revisiting goals and aims. Evaluation needs memory, and I now wonder if video and audio tape might be useful tools to help capture the essence of a discussion and bring it back to group members.

Finding the 'summing-up' process difficult, group members have been very supportive to each other. They often prompt each other; for example, if Hannah could not remember what activity she did, Peter has said, 'Didn't you play dominoes with me?'

My own part in this process is complex and bound up with collaboration with co-workers. I have particularly encouraged the summing-up process, emphasizing that this process aids the growth of the group. I can also play my part by acknowledging my power as a practitioner in the agency and my responsibility for ensuring the agency has a stake in the group. Doel and Sawdon (1999, p. 239) point out the importance of considering 'how the group meets at least some of the agency's aims, so that the findings can be fed into the agency's policy-making structures'. In social work, it often seems that groupwork is the poor relation and we plan to redress the balance by making a presentation of the group's evaluation at a special team meeting, where both the health manager and social services manager will be present. We intend to clarify how groupwork is particularly effective for people with memory problems, using the evidence gathered from the group members, and their carers. On further reflection, it would be helpful to invite group members themselves to be part of the presentation and I would like to raise this possibility with the group.

Overall, my developing understanding of group processes and the use of action techniques has, I believe, helped the group to grow from a collection of individuals to a sense of belonging in a group.

7.3 Evaluation: issues of power and oppression

I think the principal issue has been involving group members themselves in defining what 'success' is and whether the group is helping them. I've always understood the group as being more about maintenance than change; maintenance of memory, of skills, of lifestyle. Finding ways of helping people with memory problems to articulate what this means for them (and, indeed, whether 'maintenance' is their main hope for the group) is the challenge. The main dimension of discrimination is 'extent of memory' – in other words, this is what defines relative power in the group, and a person's ability to evaluate is closely related to their power of memory.

Power and Oppression

8.1 Anti-oppressive groupwork

Description

Using the notes you have been making along the way, take two specific illustrations from your groupwork (one from the early phase of the group and one from the later phase) which highlight an issue of power and oppression. Confine yourself to a description of each of the incidents or situations.

1. ILLUSTRATION FROM THE EARLY STAGE

In the first four sessions of the group, we followed the structure set out in our opening statement of purpose, where the latter part of the session was devoted to taking part in games and craft-based activities. The group members were able to choose from several options in each session. Invariably, Fred and Peter would choose to play dominoes together.

2. ILLUSTRATION FROM THE LATER STAGE

Group members were given evaluation questionnaires, which I had devised. Bella and I explained why we would like them to complete the questionnaires, and that we would explain each question in order to help them to answer. Bella gave one-to-one support to Lily and Peter, while I offered writing support to Jane, whose arthritis was bad that day.

Analysis

Consider the issues of power and oppression which were present in each of the two situations you have described. How were questions of gender, race, age, disability, sexuality, class, etc. handled?

1. ILLUSTRATION FROM THE EARLY STAGE

Although we offered choices to the group members, they had little input. The group workers devised the opening statement before the group began and we used our power to shape the group's activities. We did ask group members for their own ideas about activities, but it is debatable how able they were to exercise this choice. Older people are a marginalized group in society in that they are seen as dependent on the state for their living, and often feel that they are viewed as an unproductive burden on the economy. This can lead to passivity and to an expectation that they will be treated accordingly. Our initial offer of choice was not necessarily an empowering act, since it could have served to reinforce the gap between what older people want and what professionals perceive they need.

The choices of activity on offer were not always gender-sensitive, which perhaps explains Fred and Peter's choice of dominoes. Although it is important not to stereotype activities as male or female, it is possible that men may not expect to enjoy making candles or painting flowerpots. Bella, Wanda, June and I agonized over planning an activity programme which offered equal choices to men and women, and we did hope, perhaps unrealistically, that the two men in the group would come up with some ideas. We offered the same choice of activity to all group members, but the men declined everything except dominoes. This raises the issue of expectations of the male and female roles, dominoes being seen as an acceptable male activity, and painting and crafts as a predominantly female activity, reminiscent of knitting and basket-weaving.

Heap (1985, p.147) describes a down-spiralling chain of events, beginning with the statement that 'disability, old age, physical and mental illness and membership of minority groups compel many clients into leading very isolated lives'. He feels that these factors decrease self-esteem, which erodes an ability to function socially, and thus, in groupwork, activities need to be relevant to group members as 'self-esteem is reduced rather than enhanced by engagement in meaningless activity' (Heap 1985, p.155).

Brown (1994, p.155) describes an empowerment model for groupwork as 'the deliberate use of a group to create conditions in which members are able to regain self-esteem and more control over their own lives'. It seems that if Fred and Peter felt they were involved in an activity which had meaning for them, they would feel a sense of achievement, which would increase their self-esteem. This could be the first rung on the ladder to gaining more control over their lives. I still feel that we struggle to offer a groupwork service which meets the needs of both male and female group members, as we are four women, and this sends a message out to the group members.

On reflection, perhaps we should have verbalized our concerns to the group and tried to recruit a male co-worker. However, Fred and Peter may feel comfortable with dominoes, because they know they are competent players and because it is an acceptable 'male' activity. While we need to continue our search for gender-appropriate activities, and to keep asking group members if they have ideas of their own, we should not constantly question their choice. It is *their* choice, and the act of choosing can increase self-esteem.

2. ILLUSTRATION FROM THE LATER STAGE

Working with a model of self-directed groupwork, (Mullender and Ward 1991) I would not have devised the questionnaire, but helped the group members to construct it themselves. We handled the issue of disability in a positive way so that group members who have cognitive impairment which affects their ability to fill in forms, and group members with physical problems, were able to participate as fully as the group members who filled in the questionnaires without assistance. However, the evaluation could have been conducted using other methods, since a written questionnaire clearly discriminates against people who are unable to write for physical or cognitive reasons. The term 'disability' implies that people are not able to do something, and the emphasis of our group is on enabling group members. Although Bella and I did not want to target the group members who were unable to complete the questionnaires without assistance, in effect this happened, creating a divide between those who were able and those who were unable. Instead of feeling uncomfortable about this, we need to consider how to open this up in the group, because it is what group members experience all the time in the wider society outside our group.

In the above examples, I have discussed some of the issues of power and oppression which were present during the group's sessions. I am aware that I have not yet considered how we handled the issues of race, class and sexuality within the group. White workers must 'consciously and deliberately address race issues proactively' (Brown 1994, p.167). Our group reflects its neighbourhood, as older people in the Handley area are predominantly white and working-class. In my year at Handley Community Mental Health Team, I have only worked with white service users. However, this does not excuse the fact that we have not explicitly addressed the issue of race and discrimination in the group. Moreover, our model of four white workers could be seen as colluding with the view that white is 'normal', and this has not been challenged. Writing this portfolio has helped me to reflect on this and to consider how to address this with my co-workers. We need to find a way to consider issues of power and discrimination in a more explicit fashion, without this in turn increasing group members' sense of powerlessness.

Questions of class and sexuality have been implicit at different times in the group's life; for example, Amanda is perceived as 'different' by group members, as she dresses in suits and speaks with a West Country accent. However, I think the group has embraced this sense of difference, as Amanda has experiences to share which connect her with other group members, such as Grace and Amanda's common experience of living in big cities which were bombed during the war. Sexuality as an issue has not been raised, though preferences have been openly expressed regarding marriage and the single life.

For us as groupworkers, there is still a fear of 'holding too much power', but I believe we are beginning to understand that power itself is neither positive or negative, and that it is not a fixed quantity. Power increases as it is shared within the group.

Reflection

In what ways was your own 'biography' similar or different to group members' and what was the impact of these similarities and differences?

My personal biography at first seemed very different from the group members', but on reflection, there were many similarities. When I started working at Handley Community Mental Health Team, I was conscious of my youth, compared with the age of the service users and their carers. As a newly qualified social worker, I did not feel very confident in my own abilities, and I felt people would look at me as too young or inexperienced. As I grew in confidence and experience as a worker, I began to feel that my age was less at issue. However, I need to be sensitive to the fact that some service users and their carers find it initially disconcerting that their worker is two generations younger than they are. Once a relationship begins to build, most people see beyond initial impressions and this has been true of the group as a whole. There are many differences amongst us, but the shared aims for the group unite us.

As noted, we are four white workers, and all group members are white. Although we have not been explicit about our common 'whiteness', I have speculated what the impact would have been if there had been a black worker or member in the group, and whether our being white was important to the group members. It would be naïve to assume that race is not an issue, since we know that people look for sameness and do not necessarily know how to celebrate difference. As groupworkers, we shied away from discussion about difference, sameness and oppression, even though there were plenty of other kinds of difference to confront, such as differences in memory ability.

Our group was primarily, but not exclusively, female, reflecting to a certain extent the fact that there are more women than men employed in social care, and there are more older women than men, owing to average life expectancy. Gender was, in many ways, the main visible difference in the group, and after Fred left the only male was Peter. I would have preferred more male group members, for balance and to offer a different perspective. With hindsight, we would have liked to recruit a male groupworker, too.

Although I do not experience short-term memory problems in the way that most of the group members do, we have always emphasized that everyone has trouble remembering things sometimes, and that we all have 'abling systems'. For example, I use a diary to help me remember what I have to do. This approach means we share a problem, even if we experience it to different degrees, and look for solutions collectively; to this extent there is no 'us' and 'them'.

Class and sexuality are differences which are not necessarily obvious. I differed from most of the group members and the other groupworkers in terms of my background. Most were born and brought up in the area, in mining communities, whereas I come from north-eastern England. However, there were group members who originated from other areas, such as Amanda and Grace, and we made the most of this difference, encouraging them to reminisce about where they used to live, and reinforce their sense of identity. Issues of sexuality were not discussed, but I was careful to use language which did not assume group members were heterosexual.

I have been conscious throughout that age is the greatest and most obvious difference between the group members and me. I am younger than some of the group members' grandchildren. Age remained an issue, but I tried to be honest about the difference; for example, we spent time discussing the similarities and diferences between group members' youth and the experience of being young now. What is crucial is to have a safe forum to be able to acknowledge and celebrate these differences.

Other Perspectives

[a brief video extract is included in the original portfolio]

9.1 Video

Description

The video is set at the right point to begin viewing. The first sentence is:

> '...How we usually start these sessions off is we usually have a memory game.'
> The video extract of 10 – 15 minutes finishes with the sentence: '...You were
> thinking you wouldn't be able to remember things, but actually...'

What were your main purposes in this part of the groupwork session?

My main role in this part of the session was to facilitate the short-term memory game. I introduced the game, explaining that some members may have done the exercise before, but that it was useful in stimulating short-term memory.

In some senses, I was quite active while the group members were relatively passive. I had to walk around with the memory tray while the group remained in their chairs. While showing each group member the tray, I had to encourage them and reassure them that they *would* be able to remember if they focused on one object. Next, with my co-workers, I asked each group member if they could remember any of the objects on the tray. I acted as a facilitator in that if an individual could not remember, I opened it out to the group for support.

At the end of the game, I encouraged group members to reflect on the game and the implications of doing such an exercise in the group, asking them if they felt supported by other members, and querying whether it was easier to recall things if prompted by other people.

Analysis

How does what you see yourself doing in the video extract relate to your understanding of groupwork theory and practice? How successful are you in helping the group members to make best use of the group?

I feel that this exercise demonstrates the value of co-working, where the co-workers who are 'observing' can tune in to group members' responses and feelings. For example, Bella gives one-to-one support to a new group member who has hearing problems, and Wanda and June are able to complement my role by pointing out when other group members want to contribute to the discussion. This could also be seen as an example of the 'two clients' (Shulman 1984, pp.131–134), where I am focusing on the group, but June, Wanda and Bella are tuned in to the needs of individuals in the group.

This part of the session is quite typical of our groupwork in that we often employ action techniques in the group. This is an example of using props to aid activity and involvement. One of my aims as facilitator was to include everyone in the exercise, which is why we went round each individual, although they remained part of the large group.

Part of my reasoning behind asking individuals in turn to name an object relates to my understanding of group processes – the roles which some group members can assume. I wanted to ensure that the more dominant group members did not prevent the others from contributing but, by asking for support if a member was struggling, all members had the opportunity to help each other. This is an illustration of the interactional technique of gatekeeping.

By involving all group members in the game, I think I was successful in encouraging the group to make best use of its own resources. It generated peer support, whereby those who could best remember prompted those who could not. This extract from the session does demonstrate that group members are talking more openly about their memory problems and supporting each other – two of the aims of the group.

Reflection

With hindsight, what would you keep and what would you change from the extract you have chosen? Be specific.

Watching myself on video was unnerving and my immediate thought was that I had taken over the facilitation of the game, both from group members and from my co-workers. On reflection, I would keep my introduction to the game, as I feel this was clear and seemed to put group members at ease. I also think that two groupworkers taking the memory tray around was useful, since group members would have found it difficult to pass the tray and they needed to see it closely. I would keep my encouragement of group members to support and prompt each other, because this was felt to be very positive.

I would make some changes. I made specific reference to one of the group members in my summing up and, seeing it on the video, this seemed to put her on the spot, highlighting what she could not do rather than what she could. I think this was disempowering. I would give more time for group members to reflect on how they found the exercise; again, my viewing of the video led me to feel that one group member and I tended to dominate the summing up. I would find ways to broaden participation in this aspect of the exercise.

9.2 Report of direct observation

[An independent observer writes a brief report of observation to include in the portfolio. Past members of the 'Skills in groupwork' programme are best placed to process what they are observing, but it is by no means always possible to arrange this. The observer uses the following questions for guidance:]

Name of candidate: *Name of observer:*

Observer's relation to candidate: *Date(s) of observation:*

1. *What do you understand were the purposes of the candidate during the observed session?*

2. *How did the candidate exercise appropriate leadership in the group?*

3. *What group processes did you observe? What groupwork techniques did the candidate use?*

4. *What aspect of the group session which you observed do you consider was the most successful?*

5. *What aspect of the group session which you observed do you consider was the least successful?*

6. *Any other general or specific comments?*

9.3 The group members speak

Description

How do you think group members view 'success' in relation to this group? Describe how you found out group members' views of the group. Who were the 'stakeholders' in the group (family, friends, other professionals, etc.)? Describe how they were involved in evaluating the group. If they were not involved, why not?

For the group members, I think 'success' is not necessarily about consciously developing coping strategies, although they have all shared ways of managing their short-term memory problems, such as Grace's writing things down. I think the group is a social occasion for the group members; in particular, some of the women make a special effort with their appearance for Monday afternoons, as this could be the only time they go out in the week. It is this covert stimulation of short-term memory, the socializing and interaction, which the group members comment upon, and it is this aspect of the group which they have said they enjoy the most.

We always find out how group members have found each session, and if there is anything they would want to change. As I have already noted, this does not mean the group members would feel comfortable enough to tell us if they had not enjoyed a session. The written evaluation, also described earlier, was useful in many ways as we have tangible evidence of the positive impact of the group on the lives of its members. However, I feel the most valuable method of finding out how group members view the group is informal; this tends to be comments from the group members themselves, from carers and family, and from other workers. These comments tend to happen in the car on the way to the group, immediately after the session has finished, or when we see the group members outside the group, such as Amanda's social worker, Bella, visiting her at home.

Family members and professionals also have a stake in the group, and their informal comments indicate that the group has been helpful for them (as previously noted, Grace's community psychiatric nurse visits less, Amanda's husband has noticed fewer upsets at home). Involving these people early on, with permission to revisit later, would be a useful way of providing feedback to our group members about the way people who are important to them have experienced the impact of their participation in the group.

So far, our group has encouraged me to grow in confidence as a groupworker, and I, like the group members, look forward to Monday afternoons. It is an opportunity to enjoy the company of others, as well as learning through their experiences and having fun.

Analysis

What did group members have to say about the group? Include direct quotes or copies of written evaluations where available.

It tends to be the little, informal comments which indicate group members' true feelings about the group. With Jenny, it is the phraseology she uses when talking about the group; she sees the group in terms of 'belonging'; for example, 'There's some nice people in *our* group'. Grace and Hannah like being in the company of others: 'it beats being in the house all day'; 'I like having a chat about the old days'. Jane has also commented on the social aspect of the group and how she enjoys being with others. With Peter, it is more about actions than words, as he is a quiet group member who is more comfortable listening than contributing. However, he attends the group every week, and is always ready and waiting when we collect him. Monday afternoons are significant for him, and he is not prepared to miss them.

[Written evaluations were appended to the actual portfolio.]

Reflection

If you were to be involved in a similar group soon, what other methods might you use to help group members evaluate the impact of the group on their lives?

It would be interesting to use more art-based methods of evaluation in future groups. Certainly, I was shy of using art as a medium, and all four of us groupworkers lacked faith in our ability as artists! However, using visual rather than written methods of evaluation can be empowering for group members who struggle with literacy. This could be done either individually or as a group. For example, the group members could be encouraged to draw a picture of where they see themselves in terms of the group; this could occur halfway through the group's life, and at the end. If the group is open-ended like ours is, this exercise could take place at regular intervals, and would stand as a record of the development of the group. Although many people are horrified when asked to draw, once they have been reassured that this is not a test of artistic ability, they find it can be a liberating experience.

Another method of evaluation I would like to use is an inventory score which group members complete individually, at the beginning, and then further on in the group's life. This is like a multiple-choice questionnaire, where there are options to each question, and the group members circle the option most appropriate to them at that time, with higher ratings indicating a greater difficulty or problem. Each option is scored, and if the group has had an impact on an individual's life, it is hoped that the scores will be lower when they complete the inventory again. Care should be taken to ensure group members do not feel disempowered during the initial process; if things are bad, it can make them worse, seeing the problems so starkly. Conversely, sometimes identifying problems can help clarify them in an individual's own mind, and make it easier to address them.

In our group, group members did create tangible outcomes in the form of craft-based work, such as ceramic painting and glass-painting. These were done individually, and some group members did not take part in the activities. Doel and Sawdon (1999, p.245) describe a group product as 'a concrete outcome which speaks for itself in terms of the value of the group'. In a group like ours, the group product could be the result of everyone engaging in a particular activity; group members have suggested that at Christmas, everyone in the group could be involved in designing and making Christmas cards, and even those who do not physically make the cards could have some input as to what should go on them. The cards could be given to family and friends, and would be a concrete outcome demonstrating the value of working together as a group, and enjoying the activity. We also need to remember that Christmas can be a difficult time for some people and not everyone wants to be reminded of the festivities.

Ultimately, the best method of evaluation in groupwork is one which has been devised by the group members themselves. As groupworkers, we should work towards this, encouraging group members to be fully involved in all parts of the evaluation process, as it is *their* group, and evaluation should reflect this.

PART 3

Postscript

Chapter 6

Conclusion

Reflection on the exemplar portfolio

In Part 2 we illustrated how a recently qualified social worker used the structure of the signposted portfolio to present evidence of learning and practice in groupwork. Inevitably, readers will have formed opinions about various aspects of the work presented in the portfolio, but we need now to consider this not as a specific example but as an exemplar; in other words, to step beyond the actual illustration to what it has to tell us about the signposted portfolio as a model of learning and assessment.

There are many ways to approach this kind of deconstruction. For example, we could, in turn, use each of the three key themes of the book; learning, practice and assessment. In terms of learning, to what extent has the portfolio encouraged the novice groupworker to learn about her own practice, and does she show an ability to develop her learning? What learning styles and stages are evident from the material she presents? The learner details developments such as her increased confidence, from which we might infer successful learning, and she uses the portfolio itself to reflect on changes that she has noticed in her understanding and practice: 'Bella explained that we all had something in common – memory problems – and that we would be looking at ways of dealing with memory problems throughout the sessions of the group' (Section 3.3 - Description). The learner later reflects: 'Even using the "we" word can be tricky. Although it was true that "*we* would be looking at ways of dealing with memory problems" it was not so true that "*we* all had something in common – memory problems". It is uncomfortable using the word 'you' in those circumstances because it sets us (the group workers) apart.' (Section 4 – Power and oppression).

Groupworkers will be interested to critique the *practice* of groupwork as they see it through the prism of this portfolio. *Memory Joggers* depicts a group for people whose personal circumstances (sensory and memory impairments) challenge the scope of classic groupwork. As a result, it well illustrates the current debate in groupwork circles about the tension between 'groupwork' and 'working in groups' (Ward 1998). The portfolio allows us to see indications of both; interactions, dynamics and techniques where groupwork is used as an instrument of change, as well as examples where the group is a context of change for individuals (Ward 2000, p.52). However, describing the one as 'real' groupwork, and the other, presumably, as not, leads us into the dualist trap we described in Part 1. What is paramount is whether and how members of the group benefited from the experience, not whether the groupwork practice conformed to a stylized norm.

Ultimately, we are looking for evidence from the portfolio that the group worked, as a group and for each of the individuals, and if the learner's growing confidence and ability as a groupworker positively affected the group's development. We are concerned, too, with how well a signposted portfolio conveys the kind and quality of groupwork practice, and its flexibility with a variety of practice methods and styles.

Another way of deconstructing the exemplar is from the perspective of the assessment of professional practice. Even if we are not versed in the content matter, in this case groupwork, we can reflect on the signposted portfolio as an instrument of assessment. After all, learners are not experts in systems of assessment, yet are capable of appraising the signage in the portfolio. The portfolio's principal purpose is as an assessment document, as confirmed by the fact that no-one has yet completed a portfolio for its own sake, and all have chosen to submit it for examination. We could use the principles outlined in Part 1 to gauge the effectiveness of the exemplar in Part 2 – does it provide: an authentic fit between learning and assessment; an assessment experience which empowers the learner; and an opportunity to involve all stakeholders?

There is also the question of *level* of assessment. The signposting in itself does not indicate an explicit standard of practice. When the learner reflects openly on a dilemma, such as the example cited earlier, do we expect a certain standard of practice as well as a level of learning? The learner notes her awareness of the difficulties of using 'we' when the group leaders are in a different situation to the group members. Is it sufficient to note this kind of dilemma or should we expect evidence that it has been acted on? The dialectical approach of signposting is designed to encourage honesty in the learner's reflections, so we would not wish to inhibit this kind of candour: 'As a groupworker, I have found it difficult to "name" any of the occurrences [of Lily's self-deprecating behaviour], for fear of drawing unwanted attention to Lily, and highlighting her perceived problems.' (Section 5.1– Analysis).

However, as assessors we would be concerned if the portfolio consisted mainly of 'if only I could have …' cases. It is necessary, therefore, to balance the areas of newly acquired understanding and awareness which do not yet have a resolution, with those areas where the learner has developed new strategies and put them into practice. For example: 'From our experience of previous sessions, we learnt that some group members found it hard to contribute to games which involved general questions to the group as a whole, such as broad reminiscence or remembering things without prompts. This allowed the group to be dominated by a few members. However, with more structure, everyone could be involved' [and there are specific examples of what this meant in practice] (Section 4.1 – Analysis).

A reasonable balance of successes and failures is to be expected in the new strategies being learned and practised. The portfolio enables the learner to demonstrate a variety of developments, scattered the whole length of a 'learning–practice escalator':

An individual's learning and practice is not fixed at one particular step on the escalator, and we would expect to see evidence of developments at many different stages. Of course, assessing professional practice is not such an exact science that we can quantify the precise proportion of examples at each step. The notion of a dilemma or practice issue is itself equivocal, as is the relative significance of any two such quandaries. As explored in Part 1, the uncertain and contentious nature of professional practice means that these judgements are likely to remain as much art as science. However, we can judge an assessment system by the degree to which it helps to make the 'learning–practice escalator' transparent to both learner and assessor. Judgements about practice which is good enough, or not yet good enough, can then be related to the degree of movement on the escalator. This is a more authentic reflection of the shifting reality of professional practice than the illusion of fixed competencies.

strategy taught to others

strategy fully integrated

strategy repeated, refined

strategy tried and successful

strategy tried and failed

a hypothetical response

no developed response

awareness of dilemma or issue

unaware of dilemma or issue

Figure 9 The 'Learning–Practice escalator'

We have explored the signposted portfolio from three perspectives – learning, practice and assessment. We hope that the example in Part 2 goes some way to integrating these three perspectives into a holistic approach, using the technique of signposting. Certainly, the framework is designed to encourage learners to consider the dynamics of learning, practice and assessment and to present illustrations of all three and the relationship between them. The process of compiling the portfolio for assessment purposes is designed to improve the learning and, by implication, future practice: 'Reflecting on my rewritten section on "Attending" in the Analysis section, I realise that I focused on how I would have liked Hannah to have behaved, rather than on what I did as a groupworker…I was about to change the text in the previous section (Analysis), but decided to leave it in to give me the opportunity to demonstrate here how my understanding has developed during my work on this portfolio' (Section 5.2 – Reflection).

Those who have used the signposted portfolio have reported how it has eased the daunting task of gathering and presenting evidence of their learning and practice. Signposting teaches them to sample their practice.

Perhaps even more importantly, many have reported finding the process enhanced their learning rather than inhibited it and allowed them to express themselves creatively outside the confines of specific criteria. Paradoxically, a given structure has proved more liberating than a blank canvas.

The assessor as learner

The trio of learning, practice and assessment comes full circle when we consider that assessors are learners, too. Reading and making judgements about portfolios provides opportunities for reflection on the assessment process and the strengths and weaknesses of any particular assessment format, signposted or not. In the detail of the signposts, this leads to a consideration of how questions might be better phrased. At a broader level, are the distinctions between description, analysis and reflection apt? Sometimes, the reflection section fails to move beyond a mere elaboration of the analysis; perhaps this is a weakness in the signage, or perhaps an accurate representation of the fuzziness of the boundaries between these categories.

Just as there are learning dilemmas and practice dilemmas, so there are assessment dilemmas. For example, to what extent is a degree of repetitiveness acceptable or even unavoidable? There is some repetition in the example portfolio; is this part of the trade-off with comprehensiveness, inevitable in an instrument of assessment? For instance, the driving test is quite repetitive; you cannot expect to look in the mirror just once and tick it off as 'accomplished'. To what extent is repetition a design fault in the signposting, or a factor of the individual learner's ability to cross-reference, or to select illustrations appropriately? Assessors who are also learners ask these kinds of question and seek interim answers, demonstrating a range of positions on the learning–practice escalator.

Generic framework

The signposted portfolio has been designed so that it can be used by a variety of professionals in diverse settings. Although it evolved from two particular training programmes (groupwork and task-centred practice) in an English Social Services Department, this has proved to be a rigorous testing ground, since the learners who have compiled these portfolios have been working in a variety of settings with different service-user groups. In addition, the same portfolio structure has been presented to individual learners at varying stages of their professional lives. As the following section demonstrates, pre-qualified and post-qualified learners have responded to the same signpost questions and overall structure with about equal success, even though they are at different stages of development. Indeed, 58 per cent of all learners who led or co-facilitated a group to a successful conclusion also completed a portfolio, and about half of these were pre-qualified learners, who were not required to submit evidence for assessment. Of the portfolios submitted, 82 per cent were successful at first submission, and all of those which were resubmitted were successful in reaching the required standard (post- or pre-qualified).

Post-qualifying standards require a wider perspective and greater reference to theoretical underpinnings than pre-qualifying ones. Learners submitting a portfolio at a pre-qualified level only complete the 'description' and 'analysis' sections. However, there have been examples of work completed by pre-qualified learners which have demonstrated practices at a post-qualified level. Even within one category, such as 'post-qualified', there is a wide variety of experience and standard, as learners themselves might recognize: 'This [strong compulsion to accommodate a particular group member's needs] is partly caused by my own fear of facing conflict in the group situation, as I am a new groupworker, and I am working to overcome this fear' (Section 5.3 – Analysis).

The range of signposted portfolios completed by learners at different stages of professional development

Any identifying names have been changed; portfolio topics are presented in alphabetical order.

BASIC SKILLS GROUP

A group for five women who met for six fortnightly sessions to improve social skills and relationships.

(*Two pre-qualified learners submitted portfolios based on evidence from this group.*)

THE BOYS' GROUP

This group comprised four 13–14 year-old-boys who had been sexually abused, and were all survivors of a paedophile ring. It aimed 'to prevent what has happened to them ever happening again'.

(One post-qualified learner; co-worker did not submit a portfolio.)

CHARLTON WOMEN'S GROUP

A group to promote self-confidence and greater understanding of mental health issues among women with chronic mental health problems. The groupworkers used a feminist model of groupwork.

(One post-qualified learner and one pre-qualified learner.)

THE CHESTNUTS

A group for about twelve mentally infirm people who were socially isolated.

(Two pre-qualified learners)

GIRLS JUST WANNA HAVE FUN GROUP

A distinctly 'not therapy' group for seven to eight girls, aged 14–15 years, looking at self-esteem, sex, drugs and enjoyable activity.

(One post-qualified learner; co-worker did not submit a portfolio.)

GROUP TRAINING SESSIONS FOR NEW SUPPORT WORKERS

Group training and supervision for community support workers to 'benchmark' good working practices and to qualify for NVQ assessment and consequent salary increase.

(One pre-qualified learner)

'IT DOES MATTER' (CHANGED BY GROUP MEMBERS FROM 'WHAT MATTERS?')

A group for six to eight members focusing on mental health issues and stress management strategies.

(Two pre-qualified learners)

'LOOKING GOOD, FEELING GOOD' (CHANGED BY MEMBERS FROM 'MIRROR IMAGE')

A group to promote self-confidence and self-esteem, and a greater understanding of anxiety and ways of coping. For eight women aged 30–60 years, the group met once a week for nine two-hour sessions.

(Two pre-qualified learners)

MANAGING BEHAVIOUR FOR CARERS

This was a group of eight people who were, or were expecting to be, caring for children under 8 years old. It aimed to build on existing skills and learn tactics and strategies for dealing with challenging behaviour.

(Two pre-qualified learners)

MEMORY JOGGERS

A group for older people with mild or moderate dementia; the groupwork service was developed to meet a deficit in provision, in order to provide group stimulation and help with memory.

(One portfolio is reproduced as Part 2 of this book; the other post-qualified learner and one of the two pre-qualified learners also submitted portfolios successfully using evidence from this group.)

THE OUTINGS GROUP

A group for six people with enduring mental health problems, to develop assertiveness and sociability.

(Two pre-qualified learners)

PLUS AND MINUS GROUP

A group for 10–15 people with mental health problems who attended a day centre.

(One pre-qualified learner; co-worker did not submit a portfolio.)

SENIOR RESIDENTIAL SOCIAL WORKERS' SUPPORT GROUP

A group to help experienced residential workers to develop better services and provide mutual support and learning.

(Two post-qualified learners)

'TAG' (TEMPORARY ACCOMMODATION GROUP)

A group for young people seeking accommodation and needing preparation for independent accommodation.

(*Two post-qualified learners*)

TASK FORCE QUALITY CIRCLE

A group to facilitate team-building in a staff team working with children with learning disabilities, to explore professional issues and to improve the service to the children and their families.

(*Two pre-qualified learners*)

WOMEN OF COURAGE AND HOPE

This group brought together four women who had been sexually abused; it was planned as weekly for six weeks but actually ran for 30 sessions.

(*One post-qualified learner; co-worker did not submit a portfolio.*)

WOMEN'S GROUP

A group for six women, which met weekly for eight sessions to provide mutual support and explore women's issues.

(*One post-qualified learner; co-worker did not submit a portfolio.*)

WOMEN WITH EATING DISORDERS

A group for women with a wide range of eating disorders; this has proved to be such a successful resource that a number of different groups for women with eating disorders have been run by these groupworkers.

(*Two post-qualified learners*)

WOMEN WITH SEVERE MENTAL HEALTH PROBLEMS

This group worked towards a self-help group after the initial ten sessions facilitated by the learner. The learner also drew on some evidence from a 'Hearing voices group' run jointly with a community psychiatric nurse.

(*One post-qualified learner; co-worker, a social work student, did not submit a portfolio.*)

THE WORKSHOP GROUP

A group to develop life skills for young people who are homeless or seeking accommodation, and to help them make the transition from care to independence.

(One post-qualified learner; co-worker did not submit a portfolio.)

YOUNG PEOPLE'S GROUP

A group for young people in residential care to explore lifestyle issues, safe sex, etc.

(Two post-qualified learners)

Where co-workers in a group present a portfolio, they must each present their own individual portfolio. Though they are drawing on similar evidence (i.e. the same group), they often make very different use of it and provide distinctive perspectives.

The generic framework of the signposted portfolio is flexible enough to adapt to new standards and changing professional roles. Devolution, restructuring and the like are altering the emphasis of social work, along-side other professional groups (NISW 2000). As National Occupational Standards are revised, they could be co-opted into a signposted framework, using the language of discourse.

Critical Perspectives

What are the actual or potential problems and disadvantages of signposted portfolios?

There are a number of concerns of a practical nature, especially the issue of time. In general the material generated for inclusion in a portfolio is part and parcel of the learner's regular working life, though the groupwork portfolios are based on evidence from what is usually a new service. However, gathering, writing and reflecting on this material does require additional time for the learner, as well as the time taken by the assessors in reading, evaluating and composing feedback. The signposted portfolio is time-consuming, though its transparent structure and the availability of a growing library of examples mean that learners are better placed to estimate the size of the job. Learners and their line managers sign up to an agreement which specifies 40 hours for work on the portfolio, with an understanding that learners are likely to need additional private time. For better or worse, this has the effect of excluding potential learners whose line managers are unsympathetic or feel they cannot spare staff time.

Another practical consideration is the individual's level of computing and IT skills. There is an electronic template for the portfolio, and those able to manipulate information have an advantage. One pre-qualified learner took a course in IT specifically to help her with the portfolio, and she was delighted with this secondary gain. Not everyone feels so motivated or is in a position to improve these skills.

There are a number of technical issues, some of which we have already explored, such as repetition within the portfolio, and some overlaps between description, analysis and reflection as categories. This does not constitute a fundamental difficulty with signposting as an idea in itself, and is more concerned with refining the signage itself.

The requirement for a video excerpt can also create problems, not so much with the equipment as with issues of confidentiality. Indeed, there are circumstances, such as the group for women who had been sexually abused, where video would be an inappropriate intrusion, even if it is trained solely on the groupworkers' practice. Given most people's reluctance to use video, it could seem that these learners have been 'let off', whereas in fact they are potentially disadvantaged and must consider how to compensate for the missing dimension of video evidence in their portfolio. Other technical difficulties can arise from the need to ensure that learners have 'enough' practice, as well as the right kind, from which to draw their evidence; for example, a minimum of twelve contact hours of groupwork. However, this is a problem which is not specific to the signposted system.

There are philosophical objections to signposting. Perhaps the most significant is the view that it is 'painting by numbers', and renders the assessment task too easy or too uninventive, or both. Should learners be 'left free to use the portfolio in their own way' (Walker 1985, p.57)? We have already explored the paradox that the structure of the signposted portfolio has proved liberating rather than constraining, paradoxically freeing learners to express themselves 'authentically and spontaneously' (bell hooks 1994). What of the reproach that signage gives learners too much help? One successful learner told a group of colleagues about to embark on their portfolios that 'If you follow the questions, it writes itself.' There is a sense in which this is true, and a sense in which this is a strength of the approach. The experience of reading completed portfolios is that the signpost questions are actually very testing and expose rather than disguise weaknesses and thin responses. We need to be clear that learners are not being examined on their abilities to construct a portfolio, just as learner drivers are not judged on their proficiency at devising a test route. If anyone is to be tested in this way, it should be the authors of the assessment system!

It is also proper to raise a concern that the signposted portfolio places undue emphasis on the learner's written skills. The video excerpt and a viva interview, where the learner has an opportunity to 'talk up' the portfolio, are some compensation for those who are better at doing than writing. Learners can also use appendices imaginatively to include graphic evidence of their practice abilities (flipcharts from group sessions, etc.) In the final analysis, written skills are an essential component of good practice, and the signposted portfolio seems a fair way for them to be tested.

It is difficult to know to what extent the success of signposting is dependent on practitioners' pursuing a parallel training programme. In theory, signposts are an extremely useful guide for non-participants to gather evidence of learning and practice, but there is no doubt that the opportunity to meet other learners in workshops with tutors increases motivation and is an occasion for further learning, rehearsal and reflection. It is also a sign of the employer's commitment, not just to standards of service but also to staff development.

The most difficult question in respect of the signposted portfolio is how we find out to what extent it encourages and tests the holistic approach to learning and assessment advocated in Part 1. Does the exemplar begin to meet these ideals? We hope that you are in a better position to make this judgement having had access to a full illustration of what it means in practice. Certainly, we think that signposting has the potential to guide individual learners towards holistic assessments of their own practice and learning, while providing a direct window through which assessors can give good-quality feedback and make reliable judgements. The signage can balance specific competencies with broader contexts, and point the learner to reflect on the relationship between the two. The signpost questions elicit temporary answers and generate yet more questions in the minds and writings of competent learners. Thompson (2000, pp.68–69) has referred to this process as dialectical reasoning; 'that is, instead of trying to understand the social world in terms of fixed categories or unchanging truths, it is necessary to appreciate that social life is characterised by conflict...interaction [and] change'.

Sharing and comparing professional practice

One of the ways in which good practice can be developed is for practitioners to share their experiences. We know that it is important for learners to have access to a wide range of examples in various contexts (Garavaglia 1993), but this kind of sharing is far from routine, and Manor's (2000, p.60) observation that 'groupwork as a whole is so diverse that it is very difficult to compare and contrast practice let alone improve it' holds for other areas of practice. Proceduralized practices are more easily monitored, but professional responses to the dilemmas which procedures cannot iron out are less available. It is hoped that developments such as the Social Care Institute for Excellence (SCIE) will disseminate much-needed knowledge and information about best practices in social work and social care.

It is a challenge to know how to encourage busy practitioners to share their practice experiences in ways which are accessible to others. We believe that the signposted portfolio presents such an opportunity for coherent and studied accounts of practice, so that others can access the lessons learned; the best kind of evidence-based practice. 'Others' might be professional peers, agency managers, new learners, researchers and, indeed, service users. Peers can use signposted portfolios to compare and contrast each other's approaches to practice, groupwork or otherwise. The agency can collate data about the sum total of experience, in terms of the quality of service to its users and the continuing professional development of its staff. This information can be very important in making the wider, political case for the agency's work, and suitably anonymized illustrations of the benefits of an agency's involvement could be persuasive with funders. It is our experience that peers and managers are not yet as keen as new learners to read and learn from portfolios of practice. New learners have an immediate interest, since they are about to write their own, and the sight of actual portfolios proves reassuring. Portfolios can also provide rich detail for researchers, with proper negotiation of access and confidentiality.

As far as service users are concerned, we are really only taking the first steps to consider how they, too, might learn from practice accounts in portfolios. An interesting development has been a few instances of groupworkers in the signposted portfolio project taking the idea of portfolio (minus the assessment element) into the group itself. Group members have held their own folders, with the potential to become more of an author and less of a subject.

The signposted portfolio can be an effective vehicle to share practice learning across client groups. Participants in the groupwork programme have remarked that it is refreshing and increasingly unusual to train with people who work with different client groups, as the focus of much continuing professional development is procedural and specialized. Another feature evaluated positively is the mix of staff at different stages of their professional progression, with roughly equal participation from people with and without a professional qualification.

At a national level, portfolios are developing in different ways both within and between professional groupings; nevertheless they are based on the general principle of describing and reflecting on practice to improve it. This has potential for inter-professional learning, so that transfer of learning and practice could cross professional boundaries via the use of portfolios. The mutual accreditation of training in, say, nursing and social work is likely to accelerate this process (Bartholomew, Davis and Weinstein 1996). However, changes at a structural level are urgently needed; for example, although a school teacher successfully led a group as part of the groupwork training programme, he did not attempt a portfolio because it carried no credit within the teaching profession. On two occasions policemen applied to join the programme (to co-work groups with social workers), but on both occasions they were refused the time by their superiors. It is even less likely that they would have gained permission to complete a portfolio.

We are at an early stage in what promises to be a productive period in sharing learning and good practice in a systematic way. The principles and practice of signposted portfolios offer a way forward, as we hope the exemplar has demonstrated. In addition to paper-based media, it is likely that the internet and computer-based learning will become an increasingly significant source to compare and contrast practices, with books also incorporating CD-ROMS (e.g. Reid 2000).

Continuing professional development

During the time that we have been developing the signposted portfolio, the post-qualifying framework in social work has gradually become an established part of the fabric. Increasingly, continuing professional development is less of a hobby and more of an expectation, and this holds true across the professions. The link in some cases with pay and career advancement means that there are extrinsic pressures on all practitioners, regardless of their willingness to reflect on their practice and submit it to the scrutiny of others. In nursing, Hull and Redfern (1996, p.37) state that some practitioners argue that completing portfolios (profiling) 'actually limits choice, as it is now a compulsory element of professional development'. As sanctions are put in place against social workers who have not submitted evidence of continuing ability, there will be increasing numbers working reluctantly on portfolios, and it seems reasonable to surmise that this group will contain a higher proportion of people likely to fail the required standard. The prospect of deregistration is difficult at the best of times, even more so when vacancy rates are high.

Individual attitudes to lifelong learning cannot be divorced from team and agency culture and the profession's response to intellectual life (Jones 1996). The story of the social worker who dared not tell her team colleagues that she was studying for a degree on a part-time basis, for fear of being a laughing stock in what was a team with a strong anti-learning culture is salutary (Thompson 2000, p.155). Indeed, there are concerns that the reflective practitioner model is 'only explicitly seen when experienced practitioners are coaching neophytes – [it is] not clear if professionals actually *consistently* operate in this way' (Jones and Joss 1995, p.24; their emphasis).

The signposted portfolio is an occasion for feedback and, in most cases, celebration. 'Some jobs come with built-in opportunities for recognition to be given and job satisfaction to be enjoyed – for example, stage performers get their round of applause. However, in social work it is not so clear cut. There is much more of an onus on the individual worker to be able to recognize the successes, satisfaction and rewards of the job' (Thompson 2000, p.178). The signposted portfolio provides exactly this kind of external validation, with feedback to celebrate good practice and pinpoint areas for improvement. The groupwork portfolio also counters the tendency noted by Youll and Walker (1995, p.204) for post-qualifying courses 'to be instrumental, providing the specialist with additional knowledge and skills required to maintain existing expertise or to implement new policies and organisational arrangements'. As we have noted, signposting is a generic concept, and the groupwork example we have used is a generic practice method. The signposts themselves can be adapted for specialist practices in specialist settings.

Employability

Systems and formats for assessment must consider the broad context. In Part 1 we explored the relationship between partial and holistic approaches to learning and assessment, and the need to consider a holistic approach as one which encompasses both competence and context. A holistic view of professional education includes the release of potential as well as the acquisition of skills for a specific job (Gibbs 2000).

Clearly, professional education should guarantee the 'soft' skills as a minimum for what is often termed 'employability' – oral communication; teamworking; listening; written communication; and problem-solving (Austin Knight 1997). This means that the educational partnerships responsible for training and education must be prepared to fail learners who are not capable or suitable, while also providing qualified staff with a realistic introduction to practice, and opportunities for continuing professional development. The dualism described in Part 1 is sometimes illustrated in an unproductive antipathy between academy and agency; academy charged with an inability to prepare students for the real job and a reluctance to fail incompetent or unsuitable students, and agency accused of throwing newly qualified practitioners in at the deep end. Certainly, a novice worker needs a sound induction and beginner-level work, while agencies suffering staff shortages may struggle to provide this. Indeed, agencies under stress can displace these staffing problems onto the newly qualified arrivals, interpreting 'employability' as ability to fill the gaps left by experienced professionals. This has led some commentators to question whether employers are, indeed, themselves committed to the notion of employability (Rajan *et al.* 1999).

However, when we look closely at what all those involved are seeking, there is more accord than the caricatures suggest. Employers, educators and individual practitioners in this field want employees, graduates and colleagues who, in addition to the soft skills mentioned earlier, have the capacity to understand and work with complex situations and difficult dilemmas. Qualifying training is the opportunity to lay the foundations for this capacity, and continuing professional development serves to mature it. The problem is less about ends and more about means; how this can be delivered in the face of massive structural problems, such as student poverty and deteriorating income levels and status for human service professionals. The gap between the appropriately high standards and expectations of good practice and the falling rewards and deteriorating conditions for those expected to achieve these standards should be a matter of civic and political alarm.

Portfolios are no instrument for action at the political level. However, signposted portfolios at pre-qualifying, qualifying and post-qualifying levels do provide a good indication of competence and capacity, a window on the learner's employability and continuing employability. The ability to describe, analyse and reflect succinctly over a wide range of practice is, we believe, a fair indication of the learner's general capability. It is true that the portfolio is context-specific, as Taylor et al. (1999, p.149) note, and any one portfolio is likely to have gaps; for instance, the exemplar portfolio does not indicate knowledge of the law or the legal context of practice. Nevertheless, a range of signposted portfolios can, taken together, cover many contexts for practice. The exemplar carries only one third of the credits towards the post-qualifying award, and we would expect gaps to be satisfied in other portfolio work.

In conclusion

Social work is an intellectual activity and a practical one. This claim no doubt resonates with most other professional groups working for the public service. Any method or framework used to judge professional ability must, therefore, take the intellectual and the practical into full account. In addition to standardized expectations of good practice, we need to accommodate the learning styles and approaches of individual practitioners. By encouraging learners to speak for themselves, portfolios allow for personal expression, and the signposting model helps provide consistency in expectations about the range and scope of evidence, inviting a 'fit' between learning and assessment. This direct window can give assessors confidence in their judgements about whether the learner has achieved a required standard.

With the development of regulatory bodies such as the General Social Care Council, portfolios are likely to form part of the testimony to support practitioners' claims for registration and re-registration, or to justify that this should be withheld. In these circumstances it is important to have confidence in their ability to portray learning and practice accurately.

We need to know more about the impact of compiling a portfolio on the subsequent practice of its author. Successfully submitted and returned with feedback, is it used actively and shared with others, or does it gather dust in a drawer? With a few minor tweaks, the finished product often begs for publication in a practice journal, yet it proves hard to take that final step, even with a supportive hand. One of the biggest challenges is, therefore, how to encourage successful learners to place these accounts of their work in the public domain. Perhaps websites on the internet will be more successful than conventional print in cultivating the kind of exchange and development we have advocated in this book.

For some, it is sufficient that each individual portfolio speak for itself, no more and no less. The reader discovers the learning which an individual worker has achieved (or not) and, for instance, the impact of a group on the lives of its members. Of course, there is intrinsic value in the portfolio as a semi-private account of one person's continuing development, as well as the instrumental value in the educational and professional credit which it gives to the individual, and the protection it accords to users by monitoring standards and quality of service.

However, the extrinsic value should not be neglected. It is of utmost importance for the development of improved services, as well as more capable practitioners. Each portfolio is its own action research project, as the learner investigates and reflects on his or her practice and its impact. For agencies and employers, portfolios are a vivid album of current practices. An expanding library of portfolios provides a dynamic picture of practice which goes beyond the day-to-day documentation in case files.

The structure of the signposted model allows for comparisons and contrasts, within and between sectors of practice.

Perhaps portfolios will lead us to the long-sought grail of 'integration of theory and practice'. Certainly, there is every indication that the signposting model assists this process by the simple device of providing guidance by asking questions. It encourages learners to take out their binoculars as well as their microscopes, and readers to assess for context as well as for competence.

The opportunity to reproduce a whole portfolio is rare, but we hope that extracts from practitioners' portfolios will become a regular and integral part of future professional text books. We all have much to learn from practitioners' accounts of their experience, not least service users. We owe it to them to develop frameworks which make this a meaningful and established practice.

References

Austin Knight (1997) *Soft skills hard facts*. In collaboration with *People Management* journal. London: Austin Knight Ltd.

Ayer, A. J. (1946) *Language, Truth and Logic* (2nd edition, 17th impression). London: Victor Gollancz.

Bailey, R. and Brake, M. (eds) (1975) *Radical Social Work Practice*. London: Edward Arnold.

Bartholomew, A., Davis, J. and Weinstein, J. (1996) *Inter-Professional Education and Training in Social Work: Developing New Models*. London: CCETSW.

Benson, J. (1987) *Working More Creatively with Groups*. London: Tavistock.

Bernard, L., Burton, J., Kyne, P. and Simon, J. (1988) 'Groups for older people in residential and day care: the other groupworkers.' *Groupwork 1*, 2, 115–123.

Bertcher, H. J. (1994) *Group Participation: Techniques for Leaders and Members* (2nd edition). London: Sage.

Boud, D., Keogh, R. and Walker, D. (eds) (1985) *Reflection: Turning Experience into Learning*. New York: Nichols Publishing Company.

Boud, D. and Knights, S. (1996) 'Course design for reflective practice.' In N. Gould and I. Taylor (eds) *Reflective Learning for Social Work*. Aldershot: Arena.

Brown, A. (1992) *Groupwork* (3rd edition). Aldershot: Arena.

Brown, R. A. (1995) *Portfolio Development and Profiling for Nurses*. Salisbury: Quay Books.

Burgess, H. (1992) *Problem-led Learning for Social Work: the Enquiry and Action Approach*. London: Whiting and Birch.

Burgess, H. and Jackson, S. (1991) 'Enquiry and action learning: a new approach to social work education.' *Social Work Education 9*, 3–19.

Crimmens, P. (1998) *Storymaking and Creative Groupwork – Groupwork with Older People*. London: Jessica Kingsley Publishers.

Curnock, K. and Hardiker, P. (1979) *Towards Practice Theory: Skills and Methods in Social Assessments*. London: Routledge and Kegan Paul.

Davies, C. and Sharp, P. (2000) 'Assessment and evaluation of reflection.' In S. Burns and C. Bulman (eds) *Reflective Practice in Nursing: The Growth of the Professional Practitioner* (2nd edition). Oxford: Blackwell Science.

Davies, M. (2000) *The Blackwell Encyclopaedia of Social Work.* Oxford: Blackwell.

Doel, M and Sawdon, C. (1995) 'A strategy for groupwork education and training in a social work agency.' *Groupwork 8*, 2, 189–204.

Doel, M and Sawdon, C. (1999a) 'No group is an island: Groupwork in a social work agency.' *Groupwork 11*, 3, 50–69.

Doel, M. and Sawdon, C. (1999b) *The Essential Groupworker: Teaching and Learning Creative Groupwork.* London: Jessica Kingsley Publishers.

Doel, M. and Shardlow, S. M. (1989) *The Practice Portfolio: A Research Report.* Department of Sociological Studies, University of Sheffield.

Doel, M. and Shardlow, S. M. (1995) *Preparing Post-Qualifying Portfolios: A Practical Guide for Candidates.* London: Central Council for Education and Training in Social Work.

Doel, M. and Shardlow, S. M. (1996) 'Simulated and live practice teaching: the practice teacher's craft.' *Social Work Education 15*, 4, 16–33.

Doel, M. and Shardlow, S. M. (1998) *The New Social Work Practice.* Aldershot: Arena.

Doel, M., Shardlow, S. M., Sawdon, C. and Sawdon, D. (1996) *Teaching Social Work Practice.* Aldershot: Arena.

Dominelli, L. (1988) *Anti-Racist Social Work.* London: Macmillan.

Douglas, T. (1978) *Basic Groupwork.* London: Tavistock.

ENB (1994) *Professional Portfolio.* London: English National Board for Nursing, Midwifery and Health Visiting.

Eraut, M. (1994) '*Developing Professional Knowledge and Competence.*' Brighton: Falmer Press.

Freire, P. (1972) *Pedagogy of the Oppressed.* London: Penguin.

Garavaglia, P. L. (1993) 'How to ensure transfer of learning.' *Training and Development 47*, 10, 63–68.

George, E., Iveson, C., and Ratner, H. (1990) *Problem to Solution: Brief Therapy with Individuals and Families.* London: BT Press.

Gibbs, G. (1988) *Learning by Doing.* London: Further Education Unit, Institute of Education.

Gibbs, P. T. (2000) 'Isn't higher education employability?' *Journal of Vocational Education and Training 52*, 4, 559–571.

Goffman, E. (1967) 'Nancy Deviants.' In T. Scheff (ed.) *Mental Illness and Social Processes.* New York and London: Harper and Row.

Gould, N. and Harris, A. (1996) 'Student imagery of practice in social work and teacher education: a comparative research approach.' *British Journal of Social Work 26*, 2, 223–237.

Gould, N. and Taylor, I. (1996) *Reflective Learning for Social Work.* Aldershot: Arena.

Heap, K. (1985) *The Practice of Social Work with Groups.* London: George Allen and Unwin.

Hellman, S. (1999) 'The portfolio: a method of reflective development.' In E. Holloway and M. Carroll (eds) *Training Counselling Supervisors.* London: Sage.

Hesse, H. (1979) *Reflections.* St Albans: Triad/Panther.

Hodge, J. (1985) *Planning For Co-Leadership.* Newcastle: Tyne Ltd.

Holloway, E. and Carroll, M. (eds) (1999) *Training Counselling Supervisors.* London: Sage.

Honey, P. and Mumford, A. (1986) *The Manual of Learning Styles.* Maidenhead: Ardingley House.

hooks, bell (1994) *Teaching to Transgress: Education as the Practice of Freedom.* London: Routledge.

Huczynski, A. A. (1989) 'Training designs for organizational change.' *Management Decision 24*, 4, 27–35.

Hull, C. and Redfern, L. (1996) *Profiles and Portfolios: A Guide for Nurses and Midwives.* Houndmills: Macmillan.

Humphries, B. (1988) 'Adult learning in social work education: towards liberation or domestication?' *Critical Social Policy 23*, 8–21.

Ixer, G. (1999) 'There's no such thing as reflection.' *British Journal of Social Work 29*, 4, 513–527.

Jarvinen, A. and Kohonen, V. (1995) 'Promoting professional development in higher education through portfolio assessment.' *Assessment and Evaluation in Higher Education 20*, 1, 25–36.

Jones, C. (1996) 'Anti-intellectualism and the peculiarities of British social work education.' In N. Parton (ed) (1996) *Social Theory, Social Change and Social Work.* Routledge: London.

Jones, S. and Joss, R. (1995) 'Models of professionalism.' In M. Yelloly and M. Henkel *Learning and Teaching in Social Work: Towards Reflective Practice.* London: Jessica Kingsley Publishers.

Jordan, B. and Parton, N. (eds) (1983) *The Political Dimensions of Social Work.* Oxford: Blackwell.

Knowles, M. (1978) *The Adult Learner: A Neglected Species.* 2nd edition. Houston: Gulf.

Kolb, D. A. (1984) *Experiential Learning.* New Jersey: Prentice Hall.

Lyons, K. (2000) 'Research in social work education.' *British Journal of Social Work 30*, 4, 433–447.

Manor, O. (2000) *Choosing a Groupwork Approach: An Inclusive Stance.* London: Jessica Kingsley Publishers.

Meerabeau, J. (1992) 'Tacit nursing knowledge: an untapped resource or methodological headache?' *Journal of Advanced Nursing 17*, 108–12.

Mezirow, J. (1981) 'A critical theory of adult learning and education.' *Adult Education 32*, 3–24.

Mezirow, J. (1990) *Fostering Critical Reflection in Adulthood*. San Francisco: Jossey-Bass.

Mulcahy, D. (2000) 'Turning the contradictions of competence: competency-based training and beyond.' *Journal of Vocational Education and Training 52*, 2.

Mullender, A. (1990) 'Groupwork in residential settings for elderly people.' *Groupwork, 3*, 3, 286–301.

Mullender, A. and Ward, D. (1989) 'Challenging familiar assumptions: preparing for and initiating a self-directed group.' *Groupwork 2*,1, 5–26.

Mullender, A. and Ward, D. (1991) *Self-Directed Groupwork: Users Take Action for Empowerment*. London: Whiting and Birch.

NISW (2000) *Social Work in the Modernising Agenda*. NISW Briefing 29. London: National Institute for Social Work.

O'Hagan, K. (ed) (1996) *Competence in Social Work*. London: Jessica Kingsley Publishers.

Parton, N. (2000) 'Some thoughts on the relationship between theory and practice in and for social work.' *British Journal of Social Work 30*, 4, 449–463.

Payne, M. (1996) *What is Professional Social Work?* Birmingham: Venture Press.

Preston-Shoot, M. and Agass, D. (1990) *Making Sense of Social Work*. London: Macmillan.

Rajan, A., Van Eupen, P., Chapple, K. and Lane, D. (1999) *Employability: Bridging the Gap between Rhetoric and Reality*. Tonbridge: CREATE publishing.

Reid, W. J. (2000) *The Task Planner: An Intervention Resource for Human Service Professionals*. New York: Columbia University Press.

Reynolds, B. (1942) *Learning and Teaching in the Practice of Social Work*. New York: Rinehart & Co.

Rhodes, G. and Tallantyre, F. (1999) 'Assessment of key skills.' In S. Brown and A. Glasner (eds) *Assessment Matters in Higher Education*. Buckingham: Open University Press.

Rice, S. and Goodman, C. (1992) 'Support groups for older people – is homogeneity or heterogeneity the answer?' *Groupwork 5*, 2, 65–77.

Rogers, C. (1961) *On Becoming a Person*. London: Constable.

Sawdon, D. and Sawdon, C. (1988) 'Competence and curriculum – the practice teaching contribution.' In J. Phillipson, M. Richards and D. Sawdon (eds) *Towards a Practice-Led Curriculum*. pp.75–9. London: NISW.

Schön, D. A. (1987) *Educating the Reflective Practitioner*. San Francisco: Jossey-Bass.

Schön, D. A. (1992) 'The crisis of professional knowledge and the pursuit of an epistemology of practice.' *The Journal of Interprofessional Care 6*, 1, 49–63.

Schön, D. A. (1995) *The Reflective Practitioner*. Aldershot: Arena.

Shulman, L. (1984) *The Skills of Helping Individuals and Group* (2nd edition). Illinois: F. E. Peacock.

Sibeon, R. (1999) 'Anti-reductionist sociology.' *Sociology 33*, 2, 317–334.

Taylor, I., Thomas, J. and Sage, H. (1999) 'Portfolios for learning and assessment: laying the foundations for continuing professional development.' *Social Work Education 18*, 2, 147–160.

Thomas, M. and Pierson, J. (Eds) (1995) *The Dictionary of Social Work.* London: Collins Educational.

Thompson, N. (1993) *Anti-Discriminatory Practice.* London: Macmillan.

Thompson, N. (1995) *Theory and Practice in Health and Social Welfare.* Buckingham: Open University Press.

Thompson, N. (1998) *Promoting Equality: Challenging Discrimination and Oppression in the Human Services.* London: Macmillan.

Thompson, N. (2000) *Understanding Social Work.* London: Macmillan.

Velde, C. (1999) 'An alternative conception of competence: implications for vocational education.' *Journal of Vocational Education and Training 51*, 3, 437–447.

Walker, D. (1985) 'Writing and reflection.' In D. Boud, R. Keogh and D. Walker (eds) *Reflection: Turning Experience into Learning.* New York: Nichols Publishing Company.

Ward, D. (2000) 'Totem not token: groupwork as a vehicle for user participation.' In H. Kemshall and R. Littlechild (eds) *User Involvement and Participation in Social Care: Research Informing Practice.* pp.45–64. London: Jessica Kingsley Publishers.

Ward, D. (1998) 'Groupwork.' In R. Adams, L. Dominelli, and M. Payne (eds) *Social Work: Themes, Issues and Debates.* London: Macmillan.

Whitaker, D. S. (2000) *Using Groups to Help People* (2nd edition). London: Routledge.

Winter, R. And Maisch, M. (1996) *Professional Competence and Higher Education: The ASSET programme.* London: The Falmer Press.

Yelloly, M. and Henkel, M. (1995) *Learning and Teaching in Social Work.* London: Jessica Kingsley Publishers.

Youll, P. and Walker, C. (1995) 'Great expectations? Personal, professional and institutional agendas in advanced training.' In M. Yelloly and M. Henkel (eds) *Learning and Teaching in Social Work: Towards Reflective Practice.* London: Jessica Kingsley Publishers.

Subject Index

Author Index